The Mental Health Needs
of Looked After Children

Joanna Richardson
& Carol Joughin

FOCUS

College Research Unit

Gaskell

© The Royal College of Psychiatrists 2000, 2002.

Reprinted with amendments 2002

Gaskell is an imprint of the Royal College of Psychiatrists, 17 Belgrave Square, London SW1X 8PG.

All rights reserved. No part of this book may be reprinted or reproduced or utilised in any form or by any electronic, mechanical or other means, now known or hereafter invented, including photocopying and recording, or in any information storage or retrieval system, without permission in writing from the publishers.

Cover design by Gillian Blease, 2000.

British Library Cataloguing-in-Publication Data
A catalogue record for this book is available from the British Library.
ISBN 1-901242-48-X
Distributed in North America by American Psychiatric Press, Inc.

The views presented in this book do not necessarily reflect those of the Royal College of Psychiatrists, and the publishers are not responsible for any error of omission or fact.

Gaskell is a registered trademark of the Royal College of Psychiatrists.

The Royal College of Psychiatrists is a registered charity (no. 228636).

Printed by Henry Ling Limited, at the Dorset Press, Dorchester DT1 1HD.

Contents

"The State is My Parent..."

The state is my parent...
But it has no arms to hug me,
Or lips to kiss me,
Or ears to hear me,
Or eyes to see me.

The state is my parent...
But it leaves without saying goodbye
And tells me that I must leave without
a reason why.

The state is my parent
It must have been my fate,
Because, now just like my parent
I AM A STATE!!!!

Dedicated to Leam
(Voice for the Child in Care)

Foreword

Sir William Utting

The Children's Safeguards Review (1997) received worrying evidence of deficiencies in the childcare system. Children who are looked after by local authorities suffer as a group because of the unthinking and cruel assumption that they are at fault rather than the adults whose crimes and failings are responsible. The stigma of being 'in care' handicaps these children in gaining access to the services to which all children are entitled. They are disadvantaged in other, specific ways. Many of them have moved so often between placements that their lives have lost that stability and rhythm which children need in order to thrive. They lag far behind their contemporaries in educational attainment and have serious health needs, which in the past have often not been met. In particular, the Review received evidence that 75% of looked after children had mental health problems, some of them complex and severe.

This level of mental health difficulty is not necessarily surprising. A large proportion of these children have been abused or neglected and prevented from forming stable relationships with adults and other children. They may be disturbed both emotionally and in their behaviour. The institutionalised stigma that obstructs their use of other services applies to mental health also, but here two additional factors come into play.

The first is that child and adolescent mental health services (CAMHS) are not yet resourced to meet the needs of the whole child population. Variable coverage means that the availability of these services is further restricted in some parts of the country. Second, the professional and organisational separation between childcare and mental health has left each with only partial understanding of the other. The mental health component in childcare has consequently been under-estimated as, indeed, was the mental health component in child protection. Practitioners in childcare have not as a result always felt confident about when they should refer a child to mental health colleagues. They may also be reluctant to activate a process that in some cases may end in a psychiatric diagnosis hanging round the child's neck like an albatross and inhibiting access to other essential services.

The Government has taken steps, through the 'Quality Protects' programme and other initiatives, to remedy the most obvious deficiencies in the arrangement for bringing up children in the public care. All children entering care are to be offered a health assessment and treatment plan. A programme of targeted investment in CAMHS has begun. The National Priorities Guidance for 1999/2000 issued to the NHS and Social Services authorities sets targets for building up core child and adolescent psychiatric services.

These are bright beginnings, but establishing a comprehensive service able to respond to the total volume of need will be a lengthy process. Nevertheless, the improvements being made to the cover and quality of services encourage renewed emphasis on the importance of gaining access to them. The perceptions and judgements of the adults closest to the child are critical to this, since in the majority of cases it is they who take the initiative in seeking referral to specialist services.

For children who are looked after by local authorities, the adults closest to the child (in a sense which includes general responsibilities as well as those for direct care) are likely to be foster carers and residential and field social workers. They will find that this book builds knowledge and fortifies confidence. It presents general information about mental health conditions associated with the childcare population, illustrated by case examples and set in a context of helpful information. I recommend it also to the audience of those with wider responsibilities towards children who are looked after by local authorities. It will certainly improve their understanding of current developments in CAMHS. More importantly, it will illuminate the nature of the difficulties with which so many children in care contend, and offer signposts towards securing for them a more stable and happy life.

Acknowledgements

CONTRIBUTORS AND ADDRESSES

The FOCUS project is funded by a generous grant from the Gatsby Charitable Foundation and from Section 64 funding from the Department of Health. FOCUS would like to thank all of those listed below for their contribution to and/or their advice concerning this book. In particular we would like to thank Dr Caroline Lindsey and Dr Bob Jezzard for their help and support in its development. We would also like to especially thank the young people for allowing their poems and pieces of written work, describing their experiences and feelings about being in the care system, to be reproduced in this book.

Dr Dima Abdulrahim, Advisor, Substance Misuse Advisory Service, 46–48 Grosvenor Gardens, London SW1W 0EB.

Dr Annabelle Bundle, Associate Specialist, Community Paediatrics, Cheshire Community Healthcare Trust, Barony Road, Nantwich, Cheshire CW5 5QU.

Ms Joanne Butcher, Coordinator, Drug Education Forum, National Children's Bureau, 8 Wakley Street, London EC1V 7QE.

Dr Paul Cawthron, Consultant Psychiatrist, Nottingham Healthcare NHS Trust, Child and Adolescent Mental Health Services, Porchester Road, Nottingham NG3 6LF.

Professor Andrew Cooper, Head of Social Work, Tavistock Clinic, 120 Belsize Lane, London NW3 5BA.

Ms Judith Corlyon, Senior Research Officer, National Children's Bureau, 8 Wakley Street, London EC1V 7QE.

Professor Ilana Crome, Consultant Psychiatrist, Wolverhampton Healthcare NHS Trust, Addiction Services, Horizon House, Pitt Street, Wolverhampton WV3 0NF.

Dr Linda Dowdney, Clinical Psychologist, Course Director, Department of Clinical Psychology, University of Surrey, Guildford GU2 5XH.

Dr Eilish Gilvarry, Consultant Psychiatrist, Plummer Court, Carliol Place, Newcastle Upon Tyne, Tyne and Wear NE1 6UR.

Professor Philip Graham, 27 St Albans Road, London NW5 1RG.

Dr Hilary Griggs, Clinical Psychologist, Child and Family Services, Wrekin Hospital, Holyhead Road, Wellington, Telford TF1 2ED.

Ms Carol Halliwell, Family Therapist, Northgate Senior Clinic, Edgeware Community Hospital, Burnt Oak Broadway, Edgeware, Middlesex HA8 0AD.

Ms Meher Haque, c/o Voice for the Child in Care, Unit 4, Pride Court, 80–82 White Lion Street, London N1 9PF.

Ms Sherife Hasan, Advisor, Substance Misuse Advisory Service, 46–48 Grosvenor Gardens, London SW1W 0EB.

Professor Peter Hill, Consultant Psychiatrist, Department of Psychological Medicine, Hospital for Sick Children, Great Ormond Street, London WC1N 3JH.

Dr Sally Hodges, Clinical Psychologist, Learning Disabilities Department, Tavistock Clinic, 120 Belsize Lane, London NW3 5BA.

Dr Margaret Hunter, Child Psychotherapist, Brixton Child and Adolescent Mental Health Service, 19 Water Lane, London SW2 1NU.

Dr Robert Jezzard, Senior Advisor, Department of Health, Wellington House, 133–155 Waterloo Road, London SE1 8UG.

Dr David Jones, Consultant Psychiatrist, Park Hospital for Children, Old Road, Headington, Oxford, Oxford OX3 7LQ.

Dr Stephen Kingsbury, Consultant Psychiatrist, Health Centre, High Street, Hoddesden, Hertfordshire EN11 8BE.

Ms Helen Lewis, Senior Development Officer, National Children's Bureau, 8 Wakley Street, London EC1V 7QE.

Dr Caroline Lindsey, Consultant Psychiatrist, Child and Adolescent Department, Tavistock Clinic, 120 Belsize Lane, London NW3 5BA.

Dr Mary Lindsey, Consultant Psychiatrist, Trecare NHS Trust, 57 Pydar Street, Truro, Cornwall TR1 2SS.

Dr Adrian Marsden, Registrar, Highfield Family and Adolescent Unit, Warneford Lane, Headington, Oxon OX3 7JX.

Dr Helen Minnis, Registrar, Department of Child and Adolescent Psychiatry, Yorkhill NHS Trust, Yorkhill, Glasgow G3 8SJ.

Ms Sally Morgan, Senior Development Officer, National Children's Bureau, The Chestnuts, Spring Street, Chipping Norton, Oxfordshire OX7 5PF.

Ms Dinah Morley, Professional Services Manager, YoungMinds, 102–108 Clerkenwell Road, London EC1M 5SA.

Dr Martin Newman, Consultant Psychiatrist, William Harvey Clinic, 313–315 Cortis Road, Putney, London SW15 6XG.

Dr Paul Ramchandani, Specialist Registrar, Child and Family Psychiatric Service, Sue Nicholls Centre, Manor House, Bierton Road, Aylesbury HP20 1EG.

Dr Karen Richards, Clinical Psychologist, Department of Child and Adolescent Psychiatry, The Thelma Golding Centre, 92 Bath Road, Hounslow TW3 3EL.

Mr Peter Robinson, Psychotherapist/ Research Fellow, Young People's Unit, Tipperlinn Road, Edinburgh EH10 5HF.

Ms Kay Sargent, Lecturer in Social Work, School of Social Work, University of East Anglia, Norwich NR4 7TJ.

Professor Mike Stein, Co-Director of the Social Work Research and Development Unit, Department of Social Policy and Social Work, University of York, York YO10 5DD.

Mrs Matesebia Tadesse, Senior Child Psychologist, Askham Family Centre, 1 Askham Road, Shepherds Bush, London W12 0NW.

Ms Judy Templeton, Manager, Voice for the Child in Care, Unit 4, Pride Court, 80–82 White Lion Street, London N1 9PF.

Dr Anne Thompson, Consultant Psychiatrist, Lincoln Child and Adolescent Mental Health Service, Moore House, 10/11 Lindum Terrace, Lincoln LN2 5RS.

Mr Richard White, Partner, White and Sherwin Solicitors, Simpson House, 2/6 Cherry Orchard Road, Croydon CR0 6BA.

Dr David Will, Consultant Psychiatrist, The Young People's Unit, Royal Edinburgh Hospital, Morningside Place, Edinburgh EH10 5HF.

Mr Phil Youdan, Head of Children's Residential Unit, National Children's Bureau, 8 Wakley Street, London EC1V 7QE.

Preface

Professor Philip Graham

MENTAL HEALTH PROBLEMS IN CHILDREN AND YOUNG PEOPLE

Mental health is as important in achieving a good quality of life as physical health. Child mental health involves the absence of significant impairment of behavioural and emotional development. More positively, it also includes:

> the ability to develop psychologically, emotionally, intellectually and spiritually; the ability to initiate, develop, and sustain mutually satisfying personal relationships; the ability to become aware of others and to empathise with them; and the ability to use psychological distress as a developmental process, so that it does not hinder or impair further development. (NHS Advisory Service, 1995)

Mental health problems are common. In any one year, about one in five children will show a significant mental health problem serious enough to need help. The rate of most types of mental health problems, including depression and aggressive behaviour, has risen over the last 50 years.

Promoting mental health and dealing effectively with those with mental health problems is an important task for those concerned with all children, but especially those whose parents have had difficulties caring for them. Unresolved mental health problems cause continuing distress in the children and young people who show them, and often also impair the lives of those who care for them. Many types of problem persist into adulthood and cause continuing impairment.

Some characteristics in the child and the environment increase the child's likelihood of showing a mental health problem. These are known as 'risk factors'. They include: the child's genetic endowment, temperament and physical health; brain dysfunction; and learning difficulties; as well as family circumstances, such as inadequate parenting, emotional, physical and sexual abuse in the family, family violence, and discordant marital relationships.

Many children, even those who experience several of these risk factors, do not show emotional and behavioural problems and go on to become confident and mentally healthy adults. These children show resilience. They have effective coping strategies and often have protective factors working in their favour, such as a wide supportive network, good schooling, and adults outside the immediate family in whom they can confide. Some degree of resilience may be inborn, but much arises from circumstances that are open to change and skills that can be promoted.

There is compelling evidence (Mental Health Foundation, 1999) that looked after children often suffer from a lack of help for their mental health problems and a lack of support to promote their mental health. This book aims to provide information which will enable social workers, care workers and foster parents to develop their understanding of mental health problems and assist them to work collaboratively with families, as well as with children and young people themselves, to achieve better outcomes both now and in the future.

Part One

Looked after children

Professor Andrew Cooper

WHY DO CHILDREN COME INTO CARE?

Children come into care because somebody, usually a social worker, has assessed that at a particular point in time there is no other viable set of caring arrangements within the child's family, extended family network or community. The reasons why such an assessment is made are many and various, but it is important to stress that entry into care is always a process entailing difficult and uncertain judgements by professionals. The Children Act 1989 lays emphasis upon working 'in partnership' with parents and taking account of the wishes and feelings of children themselves. So, this means that in effect the decisions surrounding a child's entry into care should be taken in collaboration with parents and carers, and where appropriate with children themselves. The reality is that this is not always possible for all kinds of reasons – children may be too young to effectively consult, parents or carers may be in conflict with professionals about their child's needs or safety, and so on. Partnership is an important ideal, but in practice a complex and conflictual undertaking.

Once a child has entered public care, whether by agreement with their parents or carers, or as a result of a court order, the question "Why is the child in care?" is likely to take on a very different meaning in the mind of the child than it is in the minds of the adults and professionals who are now responsible for their care. Whatever leads up to the decision that a child can no longer live at home, it is very likely that they will feel that in some way it is their fault that this has happened. Feelings of bewilderment, anxiety, grief, fear and guilt are likely to be mixed up with any feelings of relief that may be appropriately present at being removed from an unsatisfactory or abusive home life. Professionals and substitute carers on the other hand may become intensely preoccupied with trying to plan for the child's future, with managing meetings, case conferences, paper work and the demands of various adult-oriented activities such as undertaking 'comprehensive assessments'. Bridging this gap between the complex responsibilities of the adult professional world and the complex emotional experience of the child's world seems to be one of the hardest things to achieve.

Children come in to care for a very wide variety of reasons. A history of physical, sexual or emotional abuse, and very commonly all three together, are present in the backgrounds of a very large proportion of such children. In the past the prevalence of a history of sexual abuse among this population of children was much less well recognised than it is now. This is important for many reasons, not least because it helps us understand why many children exhibit such very difficult behaviour within the care setting. Some children have parents who have recognised psychiatric disorders, and for many the crisis of entry into care has been preceded by an earlier crisis of marital breakdown or imprisonment of a parent. Whatever the reason much more often than not there will have been a long history of family problems often compounded by material poverty preceding the eventual entry into the care system. Thus, most children in care are recognisably 'vulnerable' in various senses by the time they enter the system. Sadly, there is much evidence that the care system may compound this vulnerability rather than increase children's resilience. About three-quarters of children leave care with no educational qualifications of any kind, and half are unemployed. Nearly a third of children in residential care at any one time are not receiving education. The recent Government 'Quality Protects' programme aims to reduce the number of moves which children experience while in care. This is important because the evidence is that nearly a quarter of children in care have moved through at least 11 placements (Shaw, 1998). Young people who have been in care seem to be a group much at risk, with around a third of young homeless people or prisoners having been in care at some point in their lives.

Psychiatric diagnoses may or may not be helpful to professionals in actually understanding the emotional predicaments and feelings of children in care. Most children will feel themselves to have been rejected even if the reality is that there was nothing their parents or carers could have done about the situation which eventually led to the breakdown of the home situation. In turn, such children are likely to reject others, making the provision of reliable and therapeutic care very difficult to provide. Understanding and listening to children is very important, but equally the recognition that difficult and challenging behaviour in some way reflects an emotional history, in which excessive problems and challenges have been visited upon the child, is terribly important. This is not a licence to allow such children to do as they please, but a request that we should recognise the depth of need within this group of children, even when the expression of this need takes quite provocative forms.

CARE OPTIONS

There are about 50,000 children in care in the UK, of whom about 11% are in residential care while 65% are fostered (Davies, 1998). Around 10,000 children are believed to be waiting for adoptive families, of whom about 13% are thought to be Black or mixed-race children (O'Hanlon & Ejioforj, 1999). This is a dramatic change in comparison with 40 years ago, when over 50% of children in care were in group homes. Over the following three decades, there were roughly equal numbers of children in both foster and residential care, but after that the proportion of those in residential care dropped to what is now the lowest level ever (Cliffe & Berridge, 1991).

Once a child enters public care then their most likely destination will be either a foster placement or a residential children's home. Over three-quarters of all looked after children are accommodated in one of these two ways, with the majority (65%) in foster care. If a child stays in care on a medium- or long-term basis, then it is possible that they may be placed with someone in the extended family, and it is quite common for this to become a permanent or semi-permanent arrangement. A smaller group of children are returned to their birth parents but with a care order still in force, so that parental responsibility is effectively shared between the local authority and the parents. This is often regarded as an unsatisfactory situation, but the Dartington Social Research Unit showed that in the end the great majority of looked after children returned to be with their families of origin after leaving care. While these children may have needed protection during their time in care, these findings reinforce the significance of the idea of working in partnership with parents (Department of Health, 1998a).

About half the 30,000 children who are newly looked after by the State each year are away from home for no more than six weeks, although 4,000 of these return for a second period of care or accommodation. Among the 15,000 children who stay longer than six weeks in care, approximately 9,500 enter foster care, and the great majority of the remainder go into residential accommodation of some kind. Intuitively, it may seem obvious that placement within a family is always preferable to placement within a children's home or institution. However, experience in practice shows that this is far from being the case. Children entering the care system have often had extremely turbulent lives from an emotional point of view, in which their personal development may have been severely disrupted, and their capacity for basic trust in other people (adults and children) severely compromised (Department of Health, 1998a).

Under these circumstances, children's challenging behaviour quickly emerges and may place adult carers under severe pressure. We can think of this as an attempt by a child or children to test out whether these adults are any more reliable and consistent than those they have previously experienced; we can also think of this behaviour as an attempt to communicate to other people what it has been like for the child in the past. But whatever perspective we take, the reality is that foster carers often find that they cannot withstand the test which a particular child or sibling group sets for them. Close attention to the individual story of how placements break down often reveals that the child almost appears to seek out the emotional vulnerabilities of the carers and to attack them in this area. While the breakdown of a placement can be disastrous and shameful for foster carers, and may confirm the child in their own sense of worthlessness, the situation should be approached with understanding and thought rather than blame and recrimination. What kind of environment or what kinds of carers might this child be in search of? Is the emotional intensity of family life too much for the child to bear at this point in their history? Might a group of committed carers within a children's home have a better chance of managing this difficult behaviour consistently and thoughtfully because they can share out the stress and strain among themselves?

These are the questions which might lead an assessment to conclude that some children, particularly those who find too much intimacy threatening or intrusive, may do better in a residential setting. Unfortunately, trends in placement provision tend to follow political or policy fashions rather than arising from a careful and systematic understanding of the emotional and material needs of the population of looked after children.

LISTENING TO CHILDREN

Perhaps the new 'Framework for the Assessment of Children in Need and their Families' (Department of Health, 1999a) will help us in this task. But often in the present climate practitioners do seem to feel as though they are overwhelmed with procedure, frameworks, guidance and forms. Used well, many of these such as the *Looking After Children* materials (Department of Health, 1995) are extremely helpful, but through all the administrative pressures and emotional demands of the job, it can be very easy to lose sight of the single most important source of information about a child's needs – what the child themself is capable of telling us.

Usually our attempts to plan and assess take place under less than ideal circumstances, where for one reason or another children have already experienced a number of placements. In some local authorities, 15% or more of looked after children undergo three or more changes of placement during a single year. For children who may already have experience of disorganised or insecure attachments this can be disastrous and only adds to the confusion of the social worker or other professional trying to make an accurate assessment of how best to help the child. A boy of seven who had been identified for adoption by his local authority had succeeded in destroying several temporary placements with his extremely difficult behaviour. In just one of them, it seemed that the foster carers really knew how to handle him, and he respected this and improved, but had to be moved on from this temporary arrangement. Suddenly, Social Services 'rediscovered' a prospective adoptive family for this boy, and moves were made in great haste to place him. Two years earlier, the couple had had a rather idealised week of caring for him and had formed the idea that they might like to adopt – in fact, they could not cope with him and the placement broke down within a week. The boy made it angrily clear to his social worker that he wished to return to the placement where he had felt safe and in fact this is what happened. The social worker felt that this was a bad thing because the child would feel that he could manipulate situations if he was sufficiently difficult and aggressive. But there was another way to see the story – the child actually knew who was best for him and his behaviour needed to be 'listened to' if a satisfactory assessment was to be made.

NEEDS OF THE 'IN CARE' POPULATION

For a whole set of reasons more to do with cultural change than professional practice, the time when 'working with children' in care involved a significant number of young babies who might be successfully placed for early adoption has now passed. The majority of children arrive in care and stay there in the context of very complex and conflicted networks of carers, birth parents, extended families, histories of substitute care and unresolved planning processes. Not all of this is to do with the failure of Social Services to plan effectively, but rather more to do with the fact that many more people (relatives, siblings, birth parents and children themselves) now have a legitimate say in a child's future; this gives more people more rights, but also makes everything more complicated and uncertain for children. Under these circumstances, 'assessment' takes on a very particular meaning and requires a very particular set of skills (Cooper & Webb, 1999).

Most children who come into the care system for any period of time either already have mental health difficulties, or are at greater risk of developing them. Finding the right 'care option', which really means the setting which can best make troubled children feel understood and recognised despite difficult behaviour and experiences, is a vital contribution to improving later-life chances and mental emotional resilience.

Why focus on the mental health needs of looked after children?

Dr Caroline Lindsey

Social workers have the responsibility for looking after some of the most disturbing and distressed young people in our society. They must also continue to address the many needs of these children's families, including the siblings, who remain at home. Foster carers need informed, skilled support to manage the often extreme challenges posed by the care of these children. Teachers, among the many other adults who come into contact with children in care, are often willing to help but want guidance as to the best way to relate to the behaviour shown by their students. These young people are suffering. What is causing the suffering and what can be done about it?

THE SIZE OF THE PROBLEM

Among the child and adolescent population as a whole, rates of mental health problems vary, but a frequently quoted figure of one in five young people reflects a significant level of disturbance. Young people in the care system have a much higher rate of mental health problems. One recent study sought social workers' views on the mental health of a group of foster children. Eighty per cent of these children were considered to require treatment from a mental health professional (Phillips, 1997). McCann *et al* (1996) showed that two-thirds of children looked after by an Oxfordshire local authority had significant psychiatric disorders. So the day-to-day experiences of working and living with these children is supported by research evidence. What, then, does it mean?

RISK FACTORS

We know that children in care are more likely to have experienced significantly more risk factors which predispose young people to develop mental health problems. These have been categorised as child, family and environmental risk factors (Pearce & Holmes, 1994). Children in the care system are, almost by definition, at risk in these ways. They have often been developmentally delayed, may be learning disabled, often have difficulty with communication and may experience failure at school. Not surprisingly, they are not always the easiest of people to get along with, which makes friendships difficult, and their self-esteem can be low. They come into care as a result of serious parental conflict and family breakdown. They may have been treated with hostility, neglect, rejection and abuse in their families. Their parents may have suffered from mental illness or have been dependent on alcohol or drugs. The young people themselves may, therefore, be genetically predisposed to develop mental health problems (Graham, 1991).

Crime and violence may have been an everyday occurrence. The theme of death and loss of significant relationships is almost always to be found in the story of the child in care. The environmental risk factors for mental health problems, which include socio-economic disadvantage and poverty, homelessness, the experience of discrimination and disaster, accurately describe the circumstances of the majority of these young people, among whom some Black and ethnic minorities are disproportionately represented.

Protective factors

Once children are received into care, there is an opportunity for some of the protective factors to come into play. There is the offer of acceptance and affection, by their carers, which may eventually lead to improved self-esteem and security. Living in good conditions, with adequate housing, food, clothing and having their needs for supervision and authoritative discipline met, are basic requirements. There is the chance to have their educational needs addressed and to build up effective communication skills. Sometimes, however, the level of disturbance makes it almost impossible for the process of recovery to begin. As Shaw (1998) found, the risk of breakdown of placements in foster care is anything between 40% and 60% and the risk of school exclusion is also very high.

Types of mental health problem

The most common disorders which these young people and those taking care of them suffer from include: anxiety, fears and depression, conduct disorder and attachment disorder. A smaller group develop serious mental illness, such as schizophrenia and bipolar affective disorder, with psychotic symptoms (which may not always be identified) in the early stages. The experience of early sexual abuse and violence may predispose some victims to become abusers themselves or to fear that they will do so. Very often the despair about their lives or the need to draw attention to their dire predicaments leads to suicidal attempts and self-harming behaviour. They may put themselves at further risk by running away, the use of drugs and alcohol, promiscuity, prostitution and criminal acts. As the vignettes later on in this book will show, the problems rarely come singly; they are complex, often severe and of long duration.

However, there are concerns about this way of thinking about the difficulties. Social workers and others are wary of labelling young people with psychiatric diagnoses. There is an understandable fear that this process further damages the frail self-esteem of young people and that it creates negative expectations in them and in those educating and taking care of them, which becomes self-fulfilling. (The issue of labelling and medicalising problems is discussed again by a family therapist on p. 80.)

Associated with these worries about labelling is the fear of stigma. It is well established that people with mental health problems are stigmatised and discriminated against in our society. These stigmatising attitudes are identifiable already in school-age children. We may then be adding the stigma of mental health difficulties to the stigma of being in care.

IMPORTANCE OF RECOGNISING MENTAL HEALTH PROBLEMS

On the other hand, the failure to identify and acknowledge significant mental health problems in a child may lead to serious difficulties in the placement. The carers may not be prepared for what they have to cope with and may not have the resources or the will to do so. They may feel that the child has been misrepresented to them. This can lead to breakdown of the placement. If problems are identified early, then carers can be offered information and support, which empowers them to deal with the situation. These young people are often very difficult to care for. They feel unlovable, rejected and despairing. They find it hard to believe that anyone wants to or is able to put up with them, least of all themselves. They are frightened by their out-of-control behaviour and their impulses to destroy relationships and themselves. Foster parents and social workers can become disheartened, depressed, angry and frustrated. They may blame themselves as well as the system. Recognition of mental health problems alleviates their personal guilt, allows them to be realistic about what can be achieved and enables them to seek help. For the young people, it may mean that they have a chance to recover.

Then there is the question of whether, having identified the problem or disorder, there is anything that can be done about it. Some professionals have been antagonistic towards what has been termed the 'medical model', in which it is seen that symptoms in an individual are treated, without taking into account the wider context. By and large, child mental health services have recognised the importance of paying heed to the contextual issues when offering assessment and interventions. In fact, it is crucial to the success of the work that the roles of all the key players in the young person's life are understood and that they are involved in the process.

Focusing on the mental health issues is important, because with the support of the social worker, the young person and the carers interventions can be made which make a difference, and which reduce disturbed and disturbing behaviour, improve relationships and make the care situation more manageable. These interventions are made at a number of levels. It is possible to support the network around the child by means of consultation, offering an understanding of the problem and strategies for management, so that the carers and professionals work together consistently to alleviate the difficulties. Foster carers and residential staff may also be offered group support. Therapeutic interventions may be offered to the young person individually, or together with his or her foster carers. There is a range of treatment options, including the use of cognitive and behavioural programmes, individual family and group therapy, medication, and combinations of these. Rarely, hospitalisation may be required. Interventions may not necessarily relieve the symptoms entirely, but may strengthen the relationships with the child, so that family life can go on. Effective intervention may reduce the risks for the future.

Unfortunately, it must also be recognised that Social Services departments (SSDs) have had great difficulty, in many parts of the country, in accessing mental health services for looked after children. Services, with their limited resources, have been reluctant to take on the complex, challenging and time-consuming work involved. Social workers in these cases change frequently, preventing continuity of care and the care plans for the young people change as well, with attempts at rehabilitation.

Nevertheless, we are now in a position where the mental health needs of children and young people have been recognised by the Government in its 'National Priorities Guidance'.

The Quality Protects initiative has made resources available for the development of mental health services for these children, and new teams are being set up around the country. Collaboration between health authorities and local authorities is now mandatory and the new child and adolescent mental health services (CAMHS) money is being shared between them.

We are in a better position than ever to focus on the mental health of looked after children.

A collaborative approach to care

FOCUS

PROMOTING AND SUPPORTING CHILDREN'S MENTAL HEALTH

Both carers and professional staff from SSDs, the National Health Service (NHS) and Education departments have responsibilities to promote and support a child's mental health. Schools that promote self-esteem and self-confidence, encourage the child to believe that they have the ability to achieve and provide a secure environment will do much to support the mental health of a child or young person. Children with mental health problems may receive help from a variety of sources from health services, such as general practitioners (GPs), or from services within education, whose primary purpose is not health. Carers for the child also have an important role to play and they should not assume that the burden of care has been taken away from them once a child has been referred to a child and adolescent mental health professional. The carer will be spending the majority time with the child and their continuing involvement and care is as important as it was before (Hunter, 1993).

The Audit Commission (1999) identified that there was a widespread lack of understanding among social work professionals of the work of many health professionals. Clearly, an understanding of the roles of professionals and agencies involved in the management of children and young people in care is very important. Since the work of the Audit Commission, reports have been produced which aim to clarify the roles of professionals who work with children and young people with mental health problems (Joughin *et al*, 1999).

Not only has there been a lack of clarity about the roles of CAMHS staff but also about how they can be approached. Figure 1 shows how staff from education, health and social services work alongside other agencies using the framework described by the NHS Health Advisory Service in 1995. This 'tiered' model for services is based on the severity of children's problems and the settings where children, young people and their families are seen and treated.

TIER 1. FRONTLINE WORKERS (WORKING IN THEIR USUAL SETTING)

This is usually the first point of contact between a child, young person, family or carer and the childcare or health agencies. The professionals in this tier include:
- GPs
- teachers
- health visitors
- social workers
- school nurses

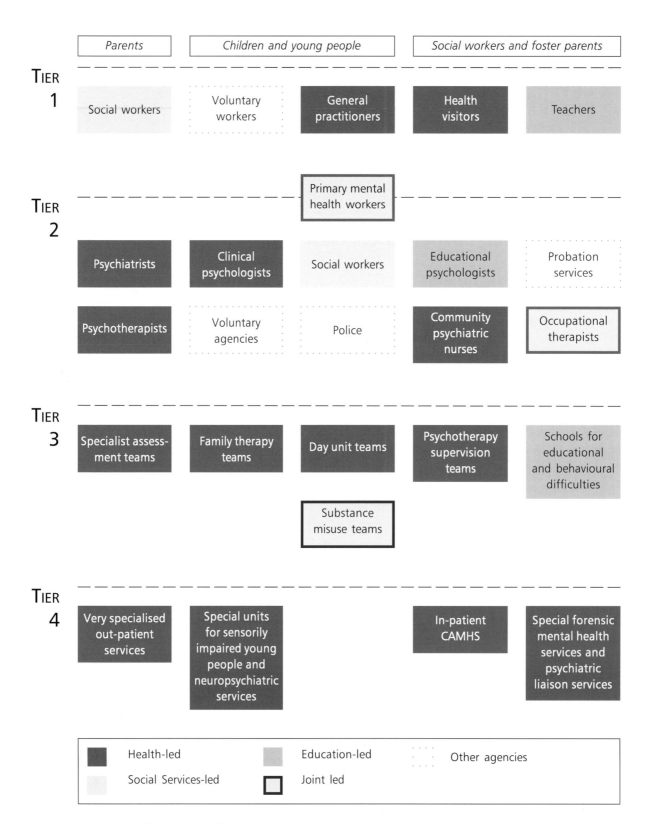

| Parents | Children and young people | | Social workers and foster parents | |

TIER 1

| Social workers | Voluntary workers | General practitioners | Health visitors | Teachers |

TIER 2

| | | Primary mental health workers | | |

| Psychiatrists | Clinical psychologists | Social workers | Educational psychologists | Probation services |

| Psychotherapists | Voluntary agencies | Police | Community psychiatric nurses | Occupational therapists |

TIER 3

| Specialist assessment teams | Family therapy teams | Day unit teams | Psychotherapy supervision teams | Schools for educational and behavioural difficulties |

| | | Substance misuse teams | | |

TIER 4

| Very specialised out-patient services | Special units for sensorily impaired young people and neuropsychiatric services | | In-patient CAMHS | Special forensic mental health services and psychiatric liaison services |

■ Health-led   ▨ Education-led   ⠿ Other agencies
▫ Social Services-led   ▢ Joint led

FIGURE 1. MULTI-AGENCY WORKING IN CHILD MENTAL HEALTH

Adapted from *Child and Adolescent Mental Health Services: Together We Stand*
(NHS Health Advisory Service, 1995)

- voluntary workers
- juvenile justice workers.

TIER 2. INDIVIDUAL SPECIALIST MENTAL HEALTH WORKERS

This is the core of CAMHS, where services are delivered by individual professionals who support Tier 1 professionals through training and consultancy. They include:
- clinical psychologists
- educational psychologists
- community psychiatric nurses
- psychotherapists
- occupational therapists
- pupil support teachers
- child psychiatrists providing consultation to agencies
- specifically tasked social workers
- paediatricians (hospital and community) and their teams.

    This work may take place:
- at the specialist service base
- in the homes and schools of the children concerned
- in health centres
- in social service establishments.

TIER 3. INTERVENTIONS OFFERED BY TEAMS OF STAFF FROM SPECIALIST CAMHS

This tier consists of more specialised services. Professionals in this tier often work in specific therapeutic teams in community child mental health clinics or child psychiatry out-patient services.

TIER 4. VERY SPECIALISED INTERVENTIONS AND CARE

This tier provides for highly specific and complex problems that require considerable resources. These include:
- in-patient psychiatric provision for adolescents
- secure provision
- specialist facilities for those with sensory handicaps
- specialised services for young people with severe eating disorders
- specialised neuropsychiatric out-patient and in-patient services
- consultations for rare paediatric disorders.

    These services are also provided by the social and education services for clients and pupils with problems of similar levels of complexity. In these circumstances, joint working and cooperation are necessary to meet the health, education and social needs of young people requiring these services.

REFERRING CHILDREN AND YOUNG PEOPLE TO CAMHS

CAMHS are not currently meeting the needs of the population. In 1996 it was estimated that only 20–30% children who had significant psychological problems received specialist professional help. The majority of children who receive professional help do not receive it from specialists but from clinicians and staff who work at Tier 1, such as GPs, health visitors and teachers.

It is important for staff in Social Services and Education to be able to call upon specialist CAMHS when necessary. In practice, the Audit Commission (1999) found that NHS clinicians provide the main referral route to the specialist CAMHS. More than half of the CAMHS referrals came from GPs (52%), and 15% from paediatricians. Only 14% came directly from Social Services and Education combined, although there was significant variation among trusts.

While some CAMHS appeared to encourage referrals from social workers, anecdotal evidence from the Audit Commission's report suggests that social workers make few referrals. They are concerned that the child or young person will have to wait a long time for an appointment and also that they will be seen in a health service clinic, rather than a setting that they are used to. This points to a need for better communication between the various sectors. All the latest Government initiatives such as Quality Protects, National Priorities Guidance and Mental Illness Specific Grants require multi-disciplinary agencies to work together for them to be a success. It is hoped that these new joint commissioning initiatives will improve access to appropriate services.

Appendix 1 of this report gives examples of innovative projects that have been set up to improve the referral process to CAMHS.

A child's view of the care system: 'forgotten children'

Meher Haque

Main topics

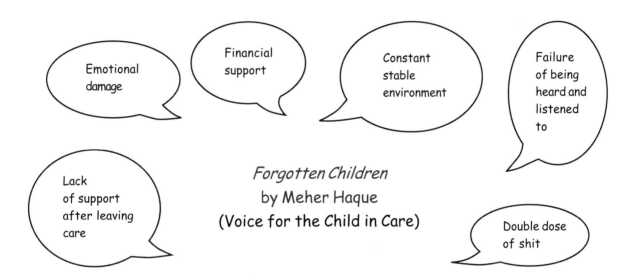

I have entitled my piece *Forgotten Children*, as it seemed to appropriately sum up how I felt as a child in care. Had I been asked what I wanted, instead of being told what other people thought I needed, my experience of being in care could have been far better than it was. Therefore, I feel the need to highlight the issues which I feel are of major concern to young people who are going through it in the future. I hope that they will be treated as individuals and not simply as statistics.

As we know, all children in care experience some degree of trauma. As a child in care, you face the stigma people tend to label you with, not to mention having to live with somebody else's family, because yours didn't work out. Every morning you wake up, you are constantly reminded of this.

These are some of the emotional difficulties that most children in care have to face:

- feeling of loss
- nobody is completely on your side
- having to change to fit in
- feeling of being abnormal
- reasons for being in care
- emotions running wild.

These are recognised to a certain extent, but not to the point where they are acknowledged – and even when they are, help is often not offered. This forces some young people to deal with their problems themselves. They are not provided with the professional help and support that is vitally needed. Often in cases like these, the young person tends to withdraw themselves from others and gradually shut themselves off from their problems, hoping that they will go away. When this happens, the problems they have had become baggage which then ends up being carried around for the rest of their lives. For some young people this leads to self-destruction. Some end up contributing to the statistics.

- 23% of adult prisoners have been in care.
- 38% of young offenders have been in care.
- 17% of young females leaving care are pregnant or already mothers.
- 30% of young single homeless people have been in care.

I myself still have a lot of issues which I need to deal with concerning my past, and even now after having left the care system, I have still not managed to sort these out.

I found that even though officials were aware of my problems that they did not push for me to talk to professionals and also failed to inform me of the importance of this.

I think that in order to improve, changes have to be made. Children and young people need to be told that there are services available to them, to support and help them. Also, they should be told what the purpose of dealing with your emotions is.

Thank you for listening.

Meher Haque is 18 years old. She was in foster care for nine years.

Part Two

Introduction to Part Two

Part Two consists of nine sections. Each section raises a number of issues relating to both social care and mental health problems that may arise for children in the care of local authorities. Each of the nine sections is laid out in the following way.

THE VIGNETTES

These have been compiled after talking with managers of children's homes, social workers and other professionals, as well as reading materials from various voluntary organisations.

The vignettes raise the issues that are then described and discussed within that section – the vignettes are intended to bring the issues to life.

The authors are aware that there are many other social issues and mental health problems affecting many children and young people in public care which are not presented within this book. Unfortunately it was not possible to include them all here.

The disclaimer following each of the vignettes reminds the reader that nearly all children and young people in local authority care have multiple problems, and these can occur in a number of combinations, not necessarily in the way that they occur in the particular vignette.

GENERAL INFORMATION

This is presented on each of the issues that are raised within the vignette. This will include, where the information is available, prevalence rates for the various problems, possible symptoms, gender differences and other relevant points.

QUESTIONS, GUIDANCE AND PROFESSIONAL COMMENT

A number of questions based on the issues raised by the vignettes are then posed. These questions were formulated after talking with social workers about what they would like to ask the professionals within child and adolescent mental health services (CAMHS). Each question was given to an appropriate professional to comment on – these included psychiatrists, psychologists, social workers and workers from voluntary organisations.

Practical suggestions in boxes appear in some of the sections. These have been compiled by psychotherapists and give suggestions concerning what a carer can do for a child or young person in their care in a crisis situation, or while they are waiting for their first appointment with CAMHS.

CHILDREN'S VOICES

These are represented by a number of poems that appear in many of the sections. These messages are from young people who have been or are still in care.

KEY READING

For each of the issues raised by the vignette, a general book or paper, where applicable, is cited, as are any relevant key secondary pieces of research.

WHAT'S GOING ON?

This will provide the reader with information on current Government policy, initiatives and research regarding the issues mentioned in each of the vignettes. There have been a number of government policies recently that will have a direct affect on the welfare of looked after children.

GOVERNMENT PROGRAMMES AND GUIDANCE

This informs the reader of the current Government policies on the various issues that are raised, setting out objectives which Social Services are required to achieve over the next couple of years.

Quality Protects (Department of Health, 1998b)

This is a major three-year programme, launched by the Department of Health in November 1998. The programme is designed to transform the management and delivery of social services for children. Working in partnership with the Department of Health, all local authorities will be expected to strengthen their management and quality assurance systems to provide safe, effective and high-quality children's services. Quality Protects is about improving the well-being of children in need, which includes: those children who are looked after by each local authority; children in the child protection system; and other children in need requiring active support from Social Services.

Quality Protects has eight main objectives, each with a number of sub-objectives. Social Services Departments (SSDs) must be able to demonstrate that they are achieving these. The sub-objectives help to define more tightly the main objectives and are accompanied by measurable performance indicators. Setting national objectives is the first step to improving the effectiveness of children's social services.

Inter-agency working with CAMHS will be required to help local authorities achieve their Quality Protects objectives, particularly those objectives aimed at improving the life chances of children in need and looked after children, and specifically those to increase placement choice and improve assessments.

National Priorities Guidance (Department of Health, 1998c)

This document enhances some of the objectives that have been addressed by Quality Protects, with the addition of specific targets. National Priorities Guidance identifies national priorities, objectives and targets for action that will bring about year-by-year improvement as part of this 10-year programme of modernisation.

Drug Misuse Special Allocation Fund (Department of Health, 1999c)

This is intended to contribute towards key objectives in the Government's anti-drugs strategy. Meeting the objectives of the strategy is a requirement of the National Priorities Guidance.

CURRENT RESEARCH AND INITIATIVES

This is intended to inform the reader of relevant projects or work being carried out in the different areas discussed, by giving examples of good or innovative practice in tackling the issues raised.

CAMHS Mental Illness Specific Grant (MISG) (Department of Health, 1999d) (recently renamed the CAMHS Innovation Mental Health Grant)

Twenty-four local authority innovative projects were first allocated a three-year grant in 1998/ 1999. The projects give good examples of joint working between Health and Social Services. Brief summaries of these projects are included in the relevant sections. Appendix 3 gives contact details for the project leads should the reader wish to find out more about a particular venture.

Other regional projects

These include any regional research project or initiative that the authors were made aware of that had been set up to investigate or help with regard to the issues. These projects vary from an academic piece of work to a voluntary organisation-led outreach project.

WHERE TO GO FOR HELP

This provides the reader with useful addresses and contact numbers for national agencies and voluntary organisations that may be of use to the carer or young person in care faced with one or more of the issues that are raised in the vignette.

"... last week, she was rushed to A & E after cutting her wrists."

Karen is 13. She has been living in a residential home for the past seven months following allegations that her stepbrother had been sexually abusing her. The alleged abuse had been taking place for the previous two years. He has not yet been prosecuted.

A social worker at the residential home is worried about Karen's behaviour as she is very flirtatious with male residents and staff, often trying to kiss and touch them. She has been found drunk on a number of occasions, and in the past month has been found twice attempting to cut herself. Last week, she was rushed to accident and emergency after badly cutting her wrists.

This vignette raises the issues of deliberate self-harm and sexual abuse. The reader is reminded that many young people in care have various problems, which can occur in a number of different combinations. Deliberate self-harm occurs in response to many different factors and not just in response to sexual abuse. Sexual abuse does not always lead to deliberate self-harm.

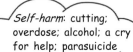
Self-harm: cutting; overdose; alcohol; a cry for help; parasuicide

GENERAL INFORMATION

DELIBERATE SELF-HARM

The term 'deliberate self-harm' is used when a person intentionally injures or harms themselves. It commonly involves self-poisoning (such as an overdose of drugs or alcohol) or self-injury (such as pulling hair, cutting, picking skin or self-strangulation). Self-poisoning is the most common form, followed by cutting (NHS Centre for Reviews and Dissemination, 1998).

Children and young people harm themselves because it is their way of dealing with complex emotions. They may feel desperate about the situation that they are in and not know how to begin to resolve their problems. Self-harm may help them to feel in control, or it may relieve extreme feelings of anger or tension.

We do know that deliberate self-harm is a risk factor for completed suicide. According to Owens & House (1994), about a quarter of all suicides attend a general hospital after a non-fatal act of self-harm in the 12 months before they die. There are no figures available on the incidence of self-harm in children and young people in care. Among the general population of adolescents who deliberately self-harm, the factors that are most likely to be associated with a higher risk of later suicide include: male gender; older age; high suicidal intent; psychosis; depression; hopelessness; and having an unclear reason for the act of deliberate self-harm. A study conducted in Oxford showed that 23% of children in the local care system suffered from major depression compared with 4% of controls (McCann et al, 1996). Clearly, self-harm needs to be taken seriously in this particularly vulnerable group of children.

SEXUAL ABUSE

Sexual abuse describes a range of activities, which includes being enticed into watching sexual acts, pornography, fondling, masturbation and sexual intercourse. Sexual abuse usually begins when children are between the ages of eight and 12 years (Monck et al, 1993).

The exact numbers of children who have been sexually abused is not known and the majority of cases are never reported. Disclosure of sexual abuse may occur quickly when the abuser is a stranger, but it may take many years for a child to disclose when the abuser is a friend or member of the family. A study by Butler & Vostanis (1998) found that 36% of girls referred to the direct-access child and adolescent mental health team had experienced sexual abuse, and 14% of girls and 11% of boys described sexual and physical abuse. This was a small study, but it gives us some idea of the numbers of children in the care system who have disclosed sexual abuse. The Health Committee Report (1998) identified abuse or neglect as being the reason for entering the care system in 20% of cases (year-end 1996). The actual number of children who have experienced sexual abuse, but not disclosed the abuse, is likely to be much higher.

Children who have been sexually abused are likely to experience behavioural problems, anxiety or depression (Merry & Andrews,1994).

(See also Section 8, which raises issues of physical and emotional abuse.)

QUESTIONS, GUIDANCE AND PROFESSIONAL COMMENT

What is the 'normal' follow-up procedure for a child or adolescent after being admitted to casualty following self-harming?

At the stage of acute presentation, emergency physical assessment and treatment as well as an initial assessment of the child's mental state is usually undertaken in the Accident and Emergency department. Following this, admission to a paediatric or adolescent ward is usually desirable (Royal College of Psychiatrists, 1998). Admission ensures that adequate physical and psychological assessments can take place and that management of crisis intervention can be planned and initiated. The admitting staff should ensure that they obtain consent to a mental

There have been a number of research studies showing that children improve over time (i.e. show fewer symptoms) with a variety of different therapeutic approaches (e.g. psychodynamic, cognitive–behavioural and group therapies), but there have been far fewer studies showing benefit of one particular therapy over another. It seems that there are features common to many therapies such as warm relationships, encouragement and education about issues of blame and responsibility that are beneficial to the children receiving these varied forms of therapy.

However, over and above this general benefit cognitive–behavioural therapy (CBT) has the strongest evidence base suggesting particular benefit in reducing behavioural problems, including sexualised behaviours in young children (Cohen & Mannarino, 1997), and emotional symptoms, such as PTSD and depression, in older childhood (Deblinger *et al*, 1996). Not all children benefit from CBT, and it may be that this smaller group needs longer-term therapy – although there is as yet no clear evidence to suggest what the best kind of therapeutic approach is for this 'treatment-resistant' group of children.

CHILDREN'S VOICES

I Feel

I feel lonely, I feel scared
Can someone please just tell me why.

I feel unhappy, I feel pressurised
Can someone please just tell me why.

I feel unloved, I feel like no one cares
Can someone please just tell me why.

I feel confused, I feel insecure
Can someone please just tell me why.

I feel I have no say in important things in my life
Can someone please just tell me why.

Ann, aged 16

'Shout to be Heard'
(Voice for the Child in Care, 1998)

It is difficult to be certain of the consequences of denying treatment to children who have been sexually abused, as the research on treatment efficacy is still patchy in its coverage, and conclusions should be drawn with appropriate caution. Indeed, it seems that some children can develop worse symptoms (particularly anxiety) over the time they are receiving therapy (Berliner & Saunders, 1996). However, we do know that these symptoms can persist (Tebbutt *et al,* 1997), and it is likely that the absence of appropriate therapeutic help leads to distressing symptoms such as low mood, anxiety, behavioural problems and inappropriate sexualised behaviours in this group of children, with serious potential long-term consequences for their functioning in spheres such as work, the forming of relationships and parenting.

Dr Paul Ramchandani and Dr David Jones

KEY READING

DELIBERATE SELF-HARM

NHS Centre for Reviews and Dissemination, University of York (1998) Deliberate self-harm. *Effective Health Care*, **4**, 1–12. (N.B. not specific to children and adolescents.)

SEXUAL ABUSE

Farmer, E. & Pollock, S. (1998) *Sexually Abused and Abusing Children in Substitute Care*. Chichester: Wiley.
Madge, N. (1997) *Abuse and Survival: A Fact File*. London: The Prince's Trust-Action.
Jones, D. P. H. & Ramchandani, P. (1999) *Child Sexual Abuse: Informing Practice from Research*. Oxford: Radcliffe Medical Press.

WHAT'S GOING ON?

GOVERNMENT PROGRAMMES AND GUIDANCE

Quality Protects and National Priorities Guidance

These documents do not refer specifically to the issues of self-harm and sexual abuse (for more information on these Government initiatives, see pp. 20–21.)

CURRENT RESEARCH AND INITIATIVES

CAMHS Mental Illness Specific Grant (MISG)

This grant was first allocated in 1998/1999 to 24 innovative projects (for more information, see p. 21).

Deliberate self-harm

We have identified two local authority projects from the 24 which seem to address the issue of self-harm.

Liverpool   Aims to help young people with serious psychological and emotional needs. The project focuses on 13–16 year olds presenting with a mixture of severe risk including overdose, self-injury, drug misuse and sexual promiscuity. An inter-agency, multi-disciplinary team provides continuous support, 24 hours a day, seven days a week.

Newham   Aims to provide a culturally sensitive counselling and outreach service to young Asian women (11–18 years of age) at risk of suicide, para-suicide and deliberate self-harm by providing support at a stage when early intervention may prove effective.

Abuse

We have identified two local authority projects from the 24 which seem to address the issue of abuse.

Dorset   Aims to provide an effective response to looked after children who have disclosed abuse, where the young person has experienced significant harm, or where there is a risk of placement breakdown. The project aims to put in place a fast-track mental health service providing a range of interventions including: art, drama and music therapies, as well as psychotherapy, counselling and group work.

West Berkshire   Aims to establish a multi-disciplinary team to focus on the mental health needs of looked after children and those who are victims of abuse, and provide assessment, consultation and direct therapeutic work.

WHERE TO GO FOR HELP

DELIBERATE SELF-HARM

National Self-harm Network
PO Box 16190, London NW1 3WW.
E-mail: nshn@wobbly.demon.co.uk
This postal service can provide information and support to people who harm themselves.
Also includes:
The Young People and Self-Harm Information Resource
Website: www.ncb.org.uk/selfharm
Provides an international listing of projects that relate to young people who physically injure themselves.

ABUSE

Family Matters
5 Manor Road, Gravesend, Kent DA12 1AA.
Tel: 01474 536661; Helpline: 01474 537392.
Provides counselling and support for survivors of sexual abuse (for adults and children over eight years old).

National Association for People Abused in Childhood (NAPAC)
c/o 42 Curtain Road, London EC2A 3NH.
A postal service for people needing information about help available to survivors of abuse.

National Society for the Prevention of Cruelty to Children
NSPCC Child Protection, 42 Curtain Road, London EC2A 3NH.
Tel: 020 7825 2500; Helpline: 0800 800 500 (24 hours); Textphone: 0800 056 0566 (24 hours).
Provides counselling, information and advice to anyone concerned about a child at risk of abuse.

GENERAL

Careline
Tel: 020 8514 1177 (Mon–Fri 10am–4pm, 7pm–10pm).
Confidential counselling for young people and adults. Can also refer callers to other organisations and support groups throughout the country.

ChildLine
Freepost 1111, London N1 OBR.
Tel: 0800 1111 (24 hours).
Provides confidential counselling, support and advice on any issue.

ChildLine for Children in Care
Freepost 1111, Glasgow G1 1BR.
Tel: 0800 884444.
A special free telephone number for children and young people who are looked after. Provides confidential counselling, support and advice on any issue.

MIND Infoline
Granta House, 15–19 Broadway, Stratford, London E15 4BQ.
Tel: 020 8522 1728 or 08457 660163 (outside London).
Provides information on all aspects of mental health and has information on self-harm.

The Samaritans
10 The Grove, Slough, Berkshire SL1 1QP.
Tel: 01753 532713; Fax: 01753 775787; Helpline: 0345 909090 (24 hours);
E-mail: jo@samaritans.org
Website: www.samaritans.org.uk
Offers free emotional support to anyone going through difficulties.

Voice for the Child in Care
Unit 4, Pride Court, 80–82 White Lion Street, London N1 9PF.
Tel: 020 7833 5792; Freephone: (for young people only) 0808 8005792.
This service offers advocacy (a voice) for children and young people in or leaving care.

YoungMinds Parents Information Service
2nd Floor, 102–108 Clerkenwell Road, London EC1M 5SA.
Tel: 020 7336 8445; Fax: 0207336 8446; Helpline: 0345 626376.
This service is for parents or carers with concerns about the mental health or emotional well-being of a child or young person. Provides information and details of local and national services.

Youth Access
2 Taylors Yard, 67 Alderbrook Road, London SW12 8AD.
Tel: 020 8772 9900; Fax: 020 8772 9746; E-mail: yaccess@dircon.co.uk
Youth Access can give details and information of counselling services in the child or young person's local area.

"… he's awaiting news of his eighth placement."

George is seven years old and of mixed parentage. His mother is White and suffers from severe depression; she often neglected George as a young child. His father is of African–Caribbean descent and left when George was a few months old. George spent most of his time from the age of two till the age of four being looked after by his grandparents. His grandmother died when he was four years old, leaving his grandfather, who was unable to care for a young child. George's mother at that time was in and out of hospital, leaving her son to be placed in a children's home for a few weeks, until a foster family could be found.

Unfortunately, George's ambivalent behaviour towards the foster parents meant that the family felt inadequate in caring for him, specifically in comforting him, as he did not reciprocate affectionate behaviour towards the family. This led to the placement breaking down.

George has since been with four other foster families and is currently back in a children's home, awaiting news of his eighth placement.

This vignette raises the issues of attachment, number of placements, ethnicity and parental mental illness. The reader is reminded that many young people in care have various problems, which can occur in a number of different combinations. Each of the issues raised whether individually or in combination with other issues, could equally cause problems for a young person.

GENERAL INFORMATION

ATTACHMENT DISORDER

Research on attachment from the developmental perspective began in the 1960s. Bowlby (1969/1982) suggested that children suffer loss when they are separated from their care-givers because of the attachments between them. Later, Bowlby (1988) found that social development was affected by later, as well as earlier, relationships. Ainsworth *et al* (1978) conducted a longitudinal investigation examining individual differences in children's use of the attachment figure as a secure base from which to explore the environment. Types of attachment between parent and child were then described.

The relationship that a child forms with their parent or first carer helps to establish a pattern of behaviours, feelings and expectations, which will affect the child's future relationships. Children with a history of neglectful, abusive or inconsistent parenting in early childhood are unlikely to develop secure early attachments or to be able to transfer this learning to form new relationships on a secure footing (Howe, 1995). If a sense of secure attachment is not formed, this may lead to the child having disordered attachments or 'attachment disorder'. The prevalence of attachment problems is unknown (Kurtz, 1996).

Two types of attachment disorder have been identified: reactive attachment disorder and disinhibited attachment disorder (World Health Organization, 1992). Children with these problems, despite being of average intelligence, are unable to make attachments to small numbers of carers.

In **reactive attachment disorder**, the child may display any of the following symptoms:

- fearfulness and hypervigilance that does not respond to comforting
- poor social interaction with peers
- aggression towards the self and others
- misery
- growth failure, in some cases.

They may show strongly contradictory or ambivalent social responses that may be most evident at times of partings and reunions.

Children with **disinhibited attachment disorder** generally have a clear early history that involved frequent changes in care-givers or multiple changes in family placements. They often appear to be unconcerned with who is looking after them, and may show any of the symptoms below:

- at two years old, clinging and non-selectively focused attachment behaviour is common; then
- at four years old, clinging tends to be replaced by attention-seeking and indiscriminately friendly behaviour; and
- in middle and later childhood, individuals may or may not have developed selective attachments, but attention-seeking behaviour often persists, and poorly modulated peer interactions are usual. There may also be associated emotional or behavioural disturbance.

ETHNICITY

There are no national data on the ethnic composition of children looked after by local authorities. We have also been unable to identify any significant research that specifically addresses the mental health needs of children from minority ethnic groups. What is clear is the need for more research into the needs, met and unmet, of these children.

PARENTAL MENTAL ILLNESS

Children who live with parents who have a mental illness have a higher risk of developing mental illness than other children (Rutter & Quinton, 1984). The Audit Commission (1999) found that 19% of children in England and Wales presenting to specialist child and adolescent mental health services (CAMHS) were living with a parent with mental illness. With some forms of mental illness, there is a risk that the child will inherit the problem through the parents' genes. However, much of the risk comes from the effects of the parents' moods or behaviour. Some forms of mental illness may prevent parents from providing the security and consistency that is necessary for a child's healthy development. There are clear associations between patterns of parenting and qualities of attachment security.

QUESTIONS, GUIDANCE AND PROFESSIONAL COMMENT

What help can a child receive for their attachment problem?

Children with attachment problems have usually experienced significant disruption in the early years of life and generally feel a profound sense of loss and insecurity. Their behaviour can be extremely challenging for both social workers and foster parents and frequently leads to a break down of placement.

It is important to provide children such as George with security, safety and continuity of care. This is ideally achieved through a successful adoption (Hodges & Tizard, 1989a), but it should be recognised that families caring for children with attachment problems may need continued support and advice in order to achieve a secure relationship with the child. Voluntary organisations run courses on parenting children with attachment difficulties. These have the additional advantage of helping families network with others in the same situation.

There is no systematic treatment research that provides a clear basis for specific treatment interventions (Wallace *et al*, 1997). However, behavioural treatment may help children to enhance their social skills and to be more discriminating when approaching familiar and strange people (Graham, 1991). CAMHS can offer various therapies, but those in which the family is actively involved in treatment, such as the parent–child game[1], may be most appropriate. Some CAMHS have, however, been reluctant to engage with children who are not in a stable placement, with the result of excluding some of the most needy children.

Dr Helen Minnis

What are the likely outcomes if a child or adolescent doesn't receive help for their attachment/ loss problems?

The answer to this question is not known at the moment. There is virtually no research into attachment disorders and there have been no longitudinal follow-up studies. There are, however, hints from other areas of research. Firstly, research on children in biological families has shown that children whose attachment style with their primary care-giver is insecure are more likely to have certain social difficulties such as aggression, anxiety and bullying (either as the victim or perpetrator). Secondly, children who have been brought up in institutions with no primary attachment figure have been shown to do less well on Intelligence Quotient (IQ)

---

[1] a therapy in which the parent is helped to interact with the child while supported by a mental health worker via an ear-bug.

tests than their family counterparts. They also show abnormal social behaviour; for example, they can be indiscriminately friendly or conversely can become withdrawn and aggressive. When these children are placed in adoptive families there is an improvement in their IQ, but some of the social behavioural problems remain (Hodges & Tizard, 1989b).

We also know that children with attachment disorder find it difficult to develop peer relationships (Troy & Sroufe, 1987). It should be noted, however, that there are many aspects of a child's experiences that may lead to this and not simply attachment problems.

Children who have experienced problems with attachment do not automatically go on to have disturbed or antisocial behaviour. Research has been carried out to examine the circumstances in which some children show 'resilience' to recover, with help, from damaging experiences (Fonagy et al, 1994). The research is still not clear regarding the issue of atwhat age it may be no longer possible to reverse the effects of disordered early attachments.

Dr Helen Minnis

The number of placements that a child or adolescent has had obviously contributes to their problems – what can be done to improve this?

The more placements that George, or any other child, has experienced, the more entrenched they may become in one (probably unsuccessful) kind of behaviour, in pursuit of a secure relationship. George's behaviour would need to be carefully assessed to be sure which pattern was predominant, but this would then offer some kind of explanation for his inability to settle easily, and to make new relationships with carers, and even for the rationale behind some of his more extreme behaviour.

There are many reasons why foster or residential placements do not work out for children. It is not always possible to match children and carers, when placements are made in a crisis, and there are often other complications like geography, educational provision, and continuing family contact. However it might be possible by focusing on relationship patterns interpreted by attachment theory to help both George and his carers to understand his behaviour better and to develop strategies to ensure that there is a better match between his own and his carers' cycles of attachment and bonding (Fahlberg, 1994).

Ms Kay Sargent

What other problems would a child like George face, coming from a mixed ethnic background, in finding a suitable placement?

It is important to think of immediate short-term and long-term goals in the placement of a child like George. In the short term, the aim should be to create a caring and safe environment in which the child's racial origin/or colour is not deemed an oddity or something special, but rather is fairly represented. Specifically, carers should consider the use of pictorial representations and educational materials, the child's body care needs and the language which is used in the child's environment. Upon entering a new placement, a child has little on which to base judgements, other than environmental or situational cues.

In the long term, identity formation should be considered. How will George begin to forge links with and establish himself as part of a given community? Questions arise like "What am I?", "What group (if any) do I belong to?", "What are the values, history, etc. of that group, and can I identify with them?" The answers may change over time and a successful placement should be supportive yet allow room for manoeuvre. Hence, supporting adults within the placement should be thinking about how to equip George with the necessary skills for successful assimilation into a given community of his choice. The dangers are that merely being 'mixed-race' may be deemed problematic by professionals (Owusu-Bempah, 1994), or that we might impose upon George a given racial identity (i.e. Black, mixed-race), thus allowing him little room to construct or align himself with any particular identity or group of his choice.

A mixed-race child of African–Caribbean and English parentage may present issues which, if not dealt with appropriately, may become problematic. We need to think of a child like George in a developmental context: he is seven years of age – at around this time, children are beginning to search out gender identification and role models. The fact that there does not appear to be a stable and consistent male figure within his life may have a negative impact – particularly when social representations of Black males are often negative. Banks (1996) talks about the absence of Black adult males from the family home of many mixed-race children. In their absence, children often become absorbed into White family networks and lose contact with Black relatives and the Black community as a whole. On the other hand, until recently many White mothers who had children by Black men were ostracised by their communities.

Box 2. Summary of factors to address when considering placements

- *Environmental*

  Is the child provided with appropriate educational material and pictorial representations? Consider the language employed and the ethnic representation of the foster family, care-giver or unit.

- *Personal*

  Are the grooming needs of the child taken care of? Does the carer know how to look after George's hair or skin? Does George have religious or dietary needs?

- *Familial*

  In accordance with the Children Act 1989, the child's wishes or views should be given full consideration. Different family members often promote and perpetuate a version of the family (and in particular the child's) history which is in keeping with their own interests and beliefs. Children whose families are in conflict can often be confused and life-story work can be very helpful in enabling the child to develop a narrative which they can process.

- *Social*

  It may be very difficult to establish and maintain social contact with a given minority community. One strategy which has been successful is the Mentoring Programme, where a positive role model is carefully selected for the child. Contact is maintained via letters, visits, phone calls, etc. The mentor becomes the door to the wider community. Community-based resources are vital sources of information and support (for both the child and placement) and they also provide a training ground for the 'practice of identity'.

They were left to raise their child without the support and knowledge to enable their child to integrate within a wider society and deal with the issue of racism. In the scenario of George, we are not told whether or not he spent his early years (age two to four) being cared for by his White or Black grandparents. This is a very important issue because it may betray his early experience of colour and difference. This experience may have significantly informed his constructions of race, his position within the family and even his understanding of the family story. We need to know what sense George makes of his history before we are able to plan specific interventions and strategies that could be employed by a placement to address potential emotional or psychological needs.

Ms Karen Richards

What messages have arisen from research regarding the effects of parental mental illness on children or adolescents?

'Mental illness' is a term that normally refers to severe psychiatric disorder such as schizophrenia, major depression or mania, overwhelming anxiety or obsessions and dementia. Much of what is discussed here, however, also applies to parents who have drug and alcohol dependency problems or disordered personality development. Indeed, these may well coexist with mental illness and further impair the parent's functioning. Having a parent with a mental illness is a powerful risk factor for mental health problems and psychiatric disorder in the child. There are various reasons for this:

- the weakening of normal parental care-giving and supervision as a consequence of the impairing effects of abnormal preoccupations, mood and concentration, which are part of most mental illness;
- distortion of parenting because of irrational concerns and attitudes, which are also part of a mental illness;
- interruption of parental care-giving by admissions of the parent to hospital;
- blunting of normal parental responsiveness to their child because of mental illness or the effects of medication;
- the child's emotional stress caused by fear for the parent's well-being, or reversed emotional dependency when the child becomes the parent's carer and feels responsible for them;
- an increased risk of discord and violence within the family, between parents and witnessed by the child or directed towards the child;
- exposure of the child to a parent's abnormal ideas about the world or to deviant examples of problem-solving skills;
- genetic influences, shared by parent and child, which cause psychiatric disorders in both;
- a higher rate of adverse life events, such as separation from the parent, parental loss of employment, re-housing, parental suicidal behaviour, teasing at school, etc.; and
- an increased likelihood of lower rates of family income and quality of housing, which further impair parental resourcefulness.

A few mental illnesses, such as severe depression, are likely to affect both parent and child, but as a general rule the form of mental health problem in the child does not necessarily follow the type of mental illness in the parent.

There is general agreement between studies that:

- roughly 33% of children referred to CAMHS have a parent with a concurrent psychiatric disorder; and
- 15–30% of children on child protection registers or received into public care have a parent with a mental illness.

It is important to note that mental illness in parents does not necessarily mean that they are bad or incompetent parents. Nor does it mean that they do not want to be good parents. For many, one of the most distressing features of their mental illness is the way in which it threatens to impair their ability to be a good parent to their child.

From the child's perspective, the presence of a mental illness in a parent can be a source of mystery and fear, not least because they are worried about growing up to develop the same problems. From what we know, children of mentally ill parents are rarely given any information about their parent's problems. Nor does it seem that much attention is paid to the fact that a number of adults with mental illness and mental health problems are also parents.

Professor Peter Hill

CHILDREN'S VOICES

Moving Placement

Moving placement is very hard
You don't run your life off a piece of card
Take this one and only chance
And go the full distance
Moving placements is very hard
So don't sit around like a lump of lard
Think ahead and start to grin
Moving placement is a place to begin
Moving placement is very hard
So don't run your life off a piece of card.

Heather, aged 12

'Shout to be Heard'
(Voice for the Child in Care, 1998)

Key Reading

Attachment disorder

Belsky, J. & Cassidy, J. (1994) Attachment: theory and practice. In *Development Through Life: A Handbook for Clinicians*, (eds M. Rutter & D.Hay), pp. 373–402. Oxford: Blackwell Science.

Howe, D., Brandon, M., Hinings, D., *et al* (1999) *Attachment Theory, Child Maltreatment and Family Support: A Practice and Assessment Model*. Basingstoke: Macmillan.

Ethnicity

Barn, R., Sinclair, R. & Ferdinand, D. (1997) *Acting on Principle: An Examination of Race and Ethnicity in Social Services Provision for Children and Families*. London: British Agencies for Adoption and Fostering.

Parental mental illness

Falkov, A. (ed.) (1998) *Crossing Bridges: Training Resources for Working with Mentally Ill Parents and their Children. Reader for Managers, Practitioners and Trainers*. London: Department of Health.

What's going on?

Government programmes and guidance

Quality Protects

This is a major three-year programme which was launched by the Department of Health in November 1998. Quality Protects is about improving the well-being of children in need, which includes those children who are looked after by local authorities (for more information on Quality Protects, see pp. 20–21).

Placement issues

Objective

> To ensure that children are securely attached to carers capable of providing safe and effective care for the duration of childhood.

There are three relevant sub-objectives for local authorities to consider, which include reducing the number of changes of main carer for looked after children and reducing the period of time for which children are looked after before they are placed for adoption.

National Priorities Guidance

This document enhances some of the objectives that have been addressed by Quality Protects with the addition of specific targets (for more information on the National Priorities Guidance, see p. 21).

Placement issues

Target

> To reduce, to no more than 16% in all authorities by 2001, the number of children looked after who have three or more placements in one year.

CURRENT RESEARCH AND INITIATIVES

CAMHS Mental Illness Specific Grant (MISG)

This grant was first allocated in 1998/1999 to 24 innovative projects (for more information, see p. 21).

Attachment and placement issues

We have identified seven local authority projects from the 24 which seem to address one or both of these issues. It should be noted that attachment problems are not the only cause of a breakdown in placements. **Causal links should not be made between these issues.**

Brighton and Hove   Aims to provide intensive assessments and treatment facilities for children with attachment difficulties who are looked after, focusing on the needs of children in, or awaiting, permanent placements with adoptive or long-term foster carers.

Cheshire   Aims to provide two small multi-agency teams, employing a range of approaches, working to help 11–16 year olds at high risk of becoming looked after owing to difficulties at home and/or school or looked after young people at risk of care and/or educational placement breakdown.

Dorset   Aims to provide an effective response to looked after children who have either disclosed abuse, where the young person has experienced significant harm, or where there is a risk of placement breakdown. The project aims to put in place a fast-track mental health service providing a range of interventions including art, drama and music therapies, as well as psychotherapy, counselling and group work.

Essex   Aims to provide rapid access and a support team for working with looked after children with significant mental health needs who are at risk of experiencing placement breakdown.

Northampton   Aims to help young people who are waiting for out-of-county placements and those failing on current placements by the introduction of a three-month intensive assessment and treatment programme.

Staffordshire   Aims to provide assessment, consultation and advice to foster parents and residential staff with regard to children with emotional and behavioural problems, hoping to increase the length of placement.

West Sussex   Aims to provide assessment and therapy to children in care with significant attachment difficulties. Also aims to provide advice and support to foster parents where mental health issues are a feature.

Ethnicity

We have identified three projects that seem to address this issue.

Newham Aims to provide a culturally sensitive counselling and outreach service to young Asian women (11–18 years of age) at risk of suicide, para-suicide and deliberate self-harm by providing support at a stage when early intervention may prove effective.

Southwark Aims to address the mental health needs of looked after children through early intervention to re-integrate children with their families, and to provide support for foster carers and services to meet the psychological needs of Black children.

Tower Hamlets A Multi-Agency Preventative (MAP) team aims to work in schools with Bangladeshi boys in need of individual and group therapy for mental health problems.

Parental mental illness

We have identified one local authority project which seems to address this issue.

Derby The project will provide flexible, community-based support to young people aged 11–17 years whose parents or other family member have a mental health problem. The project will use group-work and awareness training.

Other regional projects

Ethnicity

Bibini Centre for Young People, 60a Whalley Range, Manchester M16 8BL.
Tel: 0161 881 8558; Fax: 0161 882 0420.

The Bibini Centre takes a holistic approach to work with Black children and young people. They believe that services to young people should be tailored to the needs of the individual, therefore offering a wide range of support. They aim to meet the needs of young people experiencing mental health problems within the services offered by each of their projects. The children's home and housing project began in 1996, when a children's home was opened to provide accommodation and support to young Black people in public care. Following this, the Bibini Centre developed a housing project for young people leaving care. They have since supported a number of young people experiencing mental health problems through these projects. They also offer other support for young Black carers and family support services.

Parental mental illness

Family Welfare Association, 219 Stanstead Road, London SE23 1HU.
Tel: 020 8690 4422; Fax: 020 8690 6251.

'Building Bridges' is a support service for families where a parent is affected by mental illness. The Family Welfare Association provides services for all family members. The aims and objectives of the project are:
- to improve children's welfare and parents' mental well-being;
- to decrease disruption to families when a parent becomes mentally ill and support them through it;
- to increase knowledge, skills and collaborative working across adult mental health and child care specialisms, particularly within the London borough of Lewisham; and

- to provide a variety of comprehensive services tailored to the needs of individual families and support them over short- and long-term periods as requested by the families.

WHERE TO GO FOR HELP

ATTACHMENT AND PLACEMENT ISSUES

Adoption UK (formerly Parent to Parent Information on Adoption Services (PPIAS))
Lower Boddington, Daventry, Northamptonshire NN11 6YB.
Tel: 01327 260295; Fax: 01327 263565.
Website: www.adoptionuk.org.uk
Adoption UK aims to provide information, support and advice for prospective and existing adoptive parents and long-term foster carers. Their Attachment Support Network provides ongoing placement support and advice in dealing with behavioural and emotional difficulties within adoptive families.

British Agencies for Adoption and Fostering
Skyline House, 200 Union Street, London SE1 0IY.
Tel: 020 7593 2000; Fax: 020 7593 2001.
British Agencies for Adoption and Fostering is an organisation with a national voice promoting best practice in adoption and fostering services for children separated from their birth families.

National Foster Care Association
87 Blackfriars Road, London SE1 8HA.
Tel: 020 7828 6266; Fax 020 7620 6401; E-mail: ncfa@fostercare.org.uk
The National Foster Care Association (NFCA) is committed to raising standards of care for all children and young people who are fostered.

Post-Adoption Centre
5 Torriano Mews, Torriano Avenue, London NW5 2RZ.
Tel: 020 7284 0555; Fax: 020 7482 2367.
The Centre offers support, counselling, family work and advice – individually or in group sessions – to anyone involved in adoption. It has a daily advice line and offers training to social workers, counsellors and others working in the field of adoption.

Ethnicity

Commission for Racial Equality
Elliot House, 10–12 Allington Street, London SE1E 5EH.
Tel: 020 7828 7022; Fax: 020 7630 7605; Helpline: 0272 828 7022.
Website: www.cre.gov.uk
The Commission for Racial Equality has three main duties: to work towards the elimination of racial discrimination and to promote equality of opportunity; to encourage good relations between people from different racial backgrounds; and to monitor the way the Race Relations Act is working and recommend ways in which it can be improved.

"... his mother can no longer cope with his behaviour."

Ben is 10 years old. He has been suspended from his local school owing to his disruptive behaviour and his aggressiveness towards his peers. He has also been caught shoplifting and reported to the police three times in the past month. Ben has four younger siblings; his mother, who brings the children up alone, can no longer cope full-time with Ben's behaviour. She has threatened to walk out on her family if something is not done with Ben. He has been placed in an emergency short-term placement in a residential home.

Ben's social worker is worried about the effect of his behaviour on the other residents in the home, and feels a more appropriate placement is needed urgently. The social worker is currently discussing with Ben's school the possibility of allowing him to return.

Behavioural problems: conduct disorder; aggressive or disruptive behaviour; antisocial behaviour

This vignette raises the issues of behavioural problems, specifically conduct disorder, education and school exclusion and young offenders. The reader is reminded that many young people in care have various problems, which can occur in a number of different combinations. Each of the issues raised, whether individually or in combination with other issues, could equally cause problems for a young person.

GENERAL INFORMATION

CONDUCT DISORDER

The term 'conduct disorder' is used to describe a pattern of behaviour where there is repeated and persistent misbehaviour. This misbehaviour is much worse than is normally expected in a child of that age. It occurs in 1.5–5.6% of school-age children and 3.7–8.6% of adolescents (Kurtz, 1996). Boys are three times more likely to be affected than girls. These children and adolescents are not usually content and well-adjusted. Typically, they have low self-esteem and believe that they are bad, often showing marked misery and unhappiness as a result of a higher incidence of depression (Scott, 1998). Some of these children lack the social skills to maintain friendships and may become isolated from peer groups (Kazdin, 1995). Harsh inconsistent parenting is the major cause of conduct disorder, but hyperactivity and a low IQ may also contribute. Children with conduct disorder frequently have problems with reading.

Scott (1998) showed that five aspects of how parents bring up their children have been found repeatedly to have a long-term association with antisocial behavioural problems – poor supervision, erratic harsh discipline, parental disharmony, rejection of the child and low parental involvement in the child's activities. All children in the care system have extreme experiences of at least one of these factors and usually many more.

In young children, conduct disorder is characterised by:
- temper tantrums
- hitting and kicking people
- destruction of property
- disobeying rules
- lying
- stealing and spitefulness (Scott, 1998).

In adolescence, it may include:
- bullying and intimidation of others
- frequent fighting
- carrying and sometimes using a knife
- cruelty to people or animals
- more serious stealing
- mugging
- extensive drug misuse
- truanting from school
- running away from home and arson (Scott, 1998).

The prevalence of conduct disorder rises in adolescence and declines in early adulthood.

EDUCATION AND SCHOOL EXCLUSION

Attendance at school is a very important part of childhood as it provides the child or young person with academic and social skills and educational qualifications, which are extremely important for the competitive world of the job market (Berridge & Brodie, 1997).

The evidence from research shows that:
- as many as 75% of care leavers complete their schooling with no formal qualifications (Garrett, 1992); and
- between 12% and 19% go on to further education, compared with 68% of the general population (Biehal et al, 1995).

In order to improve the poor educational outcomes of children in care, attendance at school needs to be improved and the numbers of children who are excluded from schools needs to be reduced.

The Social Exclusion Unit (1998) reports "the permanent exclusion rate among children in care is 10 times higher than the average and as many as 30% of children in care are out of mainstream education, whether through exclusion or truancy". Reasons for this high level of exclusion include:

- the lack of a consistent adult to act as an advocate for them in contact with education;
- difficulty in concentrating at school because of problems at home;
- stigmatisation by other pupils and sometimes teachers;
- large gaps in schooling while placements are set up; and
- problems in coping with curriculum changes owing to the number of different schools attended (Morgan, 1999).

Young offenders

Crimes against individuals, such as theft, burglary and assault, increased by 73% from 1981 to 1995 in England and Wales. A disproportionate number of these crimes were committed by young people between the ages of 10 and 17 years, especially by a small number of persistent offenders. Indeed, 26% of known offenders are under 18 years of age (Audit Commission, 1996). According to Hagell & Newburn (1994), the children identified in their study as 'persistent' offenders had higher rates of contact with social services and were more likely to have come to Social Services departments' attention through supervision orders or to have been accommodated compulsorily. The Social Service Inspectorate's report (1997a) found that 23% of adult prisoners and 38% of young prisoners had been in care.

Rutter et al (1998) reported that the rate of mental health problems is high in young offenders, particularly persistent offenders. Another study by Gunn et al (1991) found a diagnosis of a primary mental health disorder in one-third of young men aged between 16 and 18 years sentenced by a court.

According to the Audit Commission (1996), three out of five young offenders who are apprehended are given a warning or caution by a police officer, but little is done to challenge their behaviour. Little or nothing happens to half of the young people proceeded against by the police: a quarter have their cases withdrawn, discontinued or dismissed; a quarter receive a conditional or absolute discharge; the remainder are given a fine, a community sentence or a custodial sentence. The effectiveness of different kinds of sentence on re-offending is often not examined. Therefore, preventing offending behaviour in the first place seems an important issue.

Factors that are associated with offending include: gender – boys are more likely to offend than girls; inadequate parenting; aggressive and hyperactive behaviour in early childhood; truancy and exclusion from school; peer group pressure to offend; unstable living conditions; lack of training and employment; and drug and alcohol abuse. These factors, according to the Audit Commission (1996), should be used to help target measures to prevent crime. These problems need to be addressed, before those at risk begin to offend.

A useful approach is 'mentoring', particularly for those young men without positive male role models in their lives. At present, this approach is being adopted and is hoped to play an important part in bail support schemes for young offenders which involve volunteer mentors.

Once young people become involved in the criminal justice system, their offending behaviour often takes precedence over developmental and mental health issues, which also need to be considered.

QUESTIONS, GUIDANCE AND PROFESSIONAL COMMENT

What management approaches are known to be effective for a child or adolescent who is difficult to control?

As Ben's case illustrates, antisocial behaviour affects the individual, the family, the school and the wider community. The widespread nature of the effects of conduct disorder provides a key to its management; evidence indicates that single, focused interventions are not particularly effective in the long term and cannot be applied to other situations. Treatments that embrace all the areas that influence and are influenced by behaviour have a greater chance of success. Thus, assessment and treatment become the responsibility of a number of agencies including teachers, social workers, psychiatrists, psychologists, GPs and community workers, and should incorporate both family members and the child or young person. Coordination of this multi-system working is the foundation of managing the problem.

The contribution of health services includes searching for, and where possible treating, physical and mental confounding factors such as epilepsy, developmental disorders, hyperactivity, alcohol and drug misuse, depression, anxiety, and the after-effects of head injury. It is also important to liaise with educational services to exclude or manage specific and general learning difficulties. These can all contribute to or result from the antisocial behaviours and have effects on the child's treatment and prognosis. Many types of treatment aimed at prevention and the subsequent management of antisocial behaviours have been tried and although sound research evidence is unavailable or inconclusive for many of the interventions there is evidence that certain approaches do seem to work.

Interventions delivered by multiple services that target each area deemed to be dysfunctional, that take into account the age of the patient, and that are delivered for long enough to make a difference have the best chance of enduring success (American Academy of Child and Adolescent Psychiatry, 1997).

Some interventions have been identified which are effective in preventing and controlling certain antisocial behaviours (Feldman *et al*, 1983). These include early community-based interventions that encourage the development of skills and social behaviour and include exposure to normal peers in mixed-sex group settings. Similar interventions in school have met with some success in terms of school performance (Lochman *et al*, 1989).

For the more disruptive younger child, multiple studies have shown that parent skills training, which embraces the positive reinforcement of desirable behaviours, together with non-violent, mild punishments for bad behaviours, is effective, in particular when combined with training for the child in the areas of problem solving, social reasoning, interpersonal sensitivity, and anger and impulse control (Webster-Stratton & Hammond, 1997). These interventions, which benefit from the active role of the parent, can be undertaken with manuals, video examples and videotaping of sessions, and can be facilitated by a therapist who does not need exhaustive training. Success is dependent in part on the motivation of the parent, which can be undermined by learning disability, psychiatric disorder, alcohol and drug misuse, emotional crises and marital discord.

As the patient moves into adolescence, interventions that are targeted at the young person and their peer group and focused on increasing the repertoire of social skills and managing anger and impulsivity can be combined with family and local community interventions.

Medication has a very limited role, but can be used to control the symptoms of coexisting conditions such as hyperactivity and significant depression, and possibly in the treatment of the extremely aggressive, institutionalised patients.

Treatment needs to be realistically balanced against resources, and in an environment where Health, Social Services, and Education are all struggling financially, requires communication, coordination, and a willingness from all three departments to share the burden of responsibility.

Dr Adrian Marsden

Looking after children such as Ben can be very demanding. They need to be provided with a secure and consistent environment. Two things are very important to remember when caring for a child like Ben. Firstly, praise good behaviour – make an effort to notice and reward socially acceptable behaviour. Secondly, be consistent with discipline. Ben needs to understand that rules are important and are there to protect his safety. Box 3 gives some examples of strategies that you may wish to use when caring for a child with behavioural problems.

Box 3. Strategies for caring for children and adolescents with behavioural problems

- **Plan ahead**. Don't make the rules up as you go along.
- **Involve the child**. Ensure they know what the rules are and why you think they are reasonable. See if the child agrees.
- **Keep rules and commands clear and brief**. If the child cannot understand they cannot obey.
- **Employ clear, quick punishments (If... then...)**. e.g. "If you don't do it now then you cannot watch TV today."
- **Be consistent**. If you don't stick to the rules the child will learn that if they ignore them you will probably give in.
- **Be calm**. Long arguments do not help.

What are the likely outcomes for a child or adolescent if nothing is done to address their conduct disorder?

Conduct disorder is responsive to treatment in young children but is very hard to eradicate in older children.

Almost half the children given a diagnosis of conduct disorder go on to develop antisocial personality disorder as an adult. A study by White *et al* (1990) found that pre-school behavioural problems were the single best predictor of antisocial behaviour at age 11. This condition is characterised by a lack of concern for the feelings of others. They exhibit irresponsible behaviour, have a disregard for social norms, rules and obligations, become easily frustrated and have a low threshold for aggression and violence. People with antisocial personality disorder show a lack of guilt, an inability to learn from experience, and a tendency to rationalise behaviours and blame others for them. Girls are more likely than boys to show depression and anxiety.

Children with conduct disorder are also thought to be at increased risk of abusing, and becoming dependent on alcohol and, to a lesser extent, illicit drugs (Offord & Bennett, 1994). They are more likely to become delinquent and engage in adult criminality. In fact, they are at risk of a widespread social dysfunction that could affect marriage, parenting, extended family, friends, work and social life. These problems are much more likely to develop if their disorder began early in life and if they have a diverse range of problem behaviours or behaviours occurring in a wide range of settings. Children who also show hyperactivity are more likely to have problems as adults. Family dysfunction, low income and parental mental illness are other factors which contribute to the risk of adult problems.

Dr Adrian Marsden

If a child or adolescent in local authority care is excluded from school, what support in their education can they expect to receive?

A decision to exclude a child from school can only be taken:
- following serious breaches of the school's discipline policy;
- once a range of alternative strategies have been tried and failed; or
- if allowing the pupil to remain in school would seriously harm the education or welfare of the pupil or of others in the school.

In all cases of more than a day's exclusion, work should be set and marked by the excluding school until either the child is reintegrated into school or is receiving other educational provision. For this temporary period, Social Services Departments (SSDs) should ensure that children in their care have somewhere suitable to do their school work, and preferably someone to support them in doing it.

Head teachers can exclude pupils, on fixed-term exclusions, for up to 45 days in a school year. However, if they exclude a child for a single block of more than 15 school days in a term, they must ensure that they (in conjunction with other relevant agencies such as the local education authority (LEA), and certainly in the case of children in public care, SSDs use the time to work out how they can help the child fit back successfully into school after that period.

They should, for example, ensure that any learning or medical needs have been (or are being) assessed and addressed. This is particularly important with children in public care, where assessments of special educational needs may well have been disrupted by lack of continuity of school and home placements. Other strategies to help reintegration (or prevent further exclusions) may include: drawing up an agreed action plan between pupil, school and parents/ carers; use of mentors; changing tutor groups; curriculum modification and involving behaviour support staff.

If a child, despite the use of such strategies, has had a series of fixed-term exclusions and/ or is thought to be at serious risk of permanent exclusion, the school should, in conjunction with Social Services, the LEA, parents and other relevant agencies, set up for the child a Pastoral Support Programme (PSP). This is a school-based, time-limited programme (e.g. 16 weeks) which aims, with the use of short-term targets, to support children in managing their behaviour better. For children in public care, the PSP should form an integral part of the care plan, with targets and outcomes being recorded, and social workers and carers aware and involved.

LEAs have a responsibility to provide suitable education (in school or otherwise) for all young people until June of the school year in which they reach the age of 16. Additionally, it is now required of local authorities that by 2002 the education provided for pupils excluded from school for more than 15 days at one time should be full-time. For pupils permanently excluded, their educational provision should be arranged by either a multi-disciplinary re-integration panel or by a named LEA officer. In either case, plans should be discussed with the parents and child, and with SSDs in the case of children in public care. A re-integration plan should be in place within a month of the governors' upholding the exclusion, and should be reviewed at least monthly.

The Government expects that most primary school-age pupils excluded from school should, with appropriate support, be re-integrated to a school within one term. However, at the other end of the spectrum, for some young people in the final two years of schooling a return to school may be unrealistic, and alternative, work-related educational packages (with appropriate involvement of the careers service) might be the best option.

Ms Sally Morgan

KEY READING

BEHAVIOURAL PROBLEMS (INCLUDING CONDUCT DISORDER)

American Academy of Child and Adolescent Psychiatry (1997) Practice parameters for the assessment and treatment of children and adolescents with conduct disorder. *Journal of the American Academy of Child and Adolescent Psychiatry*, **36** (suppl. 10).

Barlow, J. (1997) *Systematic Review of the Effectiveness of Parent Training Programmes in Improving Behavioural Problems in Children aged 3–10 years*. Oxford: Department of Public Health, Health Services Research Unit.

Webster-Stratton, C. (1993) Strategies for helping early school-aged children with oppositional defiant and conduct disorders: the importance of home–school partnerships. *School Psychology Review*, **22**, 437–457.

EDUCATION

Morgan, S. (1999) *Care about Education: A Joint Training Curriculum for Supporting Children in Public Care*. London: National Children's Bureau.

Who's Going To Listen?

I made a complaint about last week
And I've heard nothing back not even a squeak.

So now I might as well live life on, while the
Staff nag nag on.
I'll sit here and think, 'Some day I'll be gone'.

They have their good days
They have their bad

They say I have attitude
And then they get mad

Then they stop listening
And that makes me sad.

So what can I do to be understood?
Try to speak nicely and try to be good?
Or just be myself and say what I mean

And cut out the swearing and keep it all clean.
Then maybe they'll listen then things will change

Then my life will get better and things rearrange.

Matthew, aged 15.

'Shout to be Heard'
(Voice for the Child in Care, 1998)

What's going on?

GOVERNMENT PROGRAMMES AND GUIDANCE

Quality Protects

This is a major three-year programme, which was launched by the Department of Health in November 1998. Quality Protects is about improving the well-being of children in need, which includes those children who are looked after by local authorities (for more information on Quality Protects, see pp. 20–21).

Education

Objective

> To ensure that children looked after gain maximum life chance benefits from educational opportunities, health care and social care.

There is a relevant sub-objective for local authorities to deliver on, which is to bring the overall performance of children looked after for a year or more closer into line with local children generally at key stage SATs and GCSE.

Young offenders

Another sub-objective is one related to young offenders:

> To reduce the rate of offending of children looked after closer to the level for all children of the same age living in the same area.

National Priorities Guidance

This document enhances some of the objectives which have been addressed by Quality Protects by the addition of specific targets (for more information on the National Priorities Guidance, see p. 21).

Education

Targets

> To improve the educational attainment of children looked after, by increasing to at least 50% by 2001 the proportion of children leaving care at 16 or later with a GCSE of GNVQ qualification; and to 75% by 2003.

> To demonstrate that the level of employment, training or education amongst young people aged 19 in 2001/02 who were looked after by Local Authorities in their 17th year on 1st April 1999, is at least 60% of the level amongst all young people of the same age in their area.

Young offenders

Target

> To set up new structures for work with young offenders under the Crime and Disorder Act. Multi-agency youth offending teams are to be established by Local Authorities with social services and education responsibilities, in partnership with Health Authorities, the police and probation service.

New draft guidance on 'The Education of Children being Looked After by Local Authorities' was issued by the Department for Education and Employment and the Department of Health (1999). Subject to consultation and ministerial approval, a number of measures (some of them statutory) are being introduced this year, aimed at improving educational outcomes for children and young people in care. These proposals include:

- the local authority having a policy on the education of children in public care, setting out the children's entitlement to full-time education in mainstream school, wherever possible, and how they and their carers can access support, when necessary;
- a designated teacher in every school with responsibility for children in public care;
- a personal education plan for every child;
- care placements to be made only with education provision secured (unless excepted on health and safety grounds); and
- a time limit of 30 days for local authorities to secure an education placement for children.

CURRENT RESEARCH AND INITIATIVES

CAMHS Mental Illness Specific Grant (MISG)

This grant was first allocated in 1998/1999 to 24 innovative projects (for more information, see p. 21).

Behavioural problems

We have identified five projects from the 24 which examine the issue of behavioural problems.

Cornwall   Aims to establish structured behavioural modification plans for young children through the use of parenting groups to support family–school relationships and parenting skills.

Leicester   Aims to provide specialist advice, consultation, support and guidance for families of children exhibiting behavioural difficulties in the community.

Norfolk   Aims to help children and young people who are vulnerable, have problems managing their behaviour and have emerging anxiety symptoms. This project will involve multi-disciplinary Tier 2 teams based in three primary care groups.

Southampton   Aims to provide crisis intervention and behavioural support for children and young people with complex mental health and extreme behavioural difficulties by means of coordinated and consistent inputs from health, social services and education professionals.

Staffordshire   Aims to provide timely, consistent professional support (assessment, consultation and advice) to carers of children and young people, including some with challenging behaviour, looked after by the local authority.

Education

We have identified three local authority projects from the 24 which seem to address the issues of education and school exclusion.

Bury and Rochdale   Aims to work to help all excluded children, and those children under immediate threat of exclusion, aged between four and 12 years old, by providing school and home support.

City of York and North Yorkshire   Aims to provide school-based multi-agency support services for young people with emotional and behavioural disturbance who are at risk of exclusion.

Tower Hamlets   Aims to provide a Multi-Agency Preventative (MAP) team to work in schools with Bangladeshi boys in need of individual and group therapy for mental health problems.

Young offenders

We have identified two projects from the 24 which highlight the issue of young offenders.

Devon   Aims to provide and evaluate a range of mental health services to support the work of a youth offending team and regional secure unit in assessing and treating the significant mental health needs of troubled young people.

Lewisham   Aims to provide direct intervention for young offenders and those at risk of offending with mental health needs and substance misuse problems who will not engage with Tier 3 services.

Other regional projects

Education

The Equal Chances project will provide local authorities with tools to improve the educational opportunities and outcomes of looked after children and young people. The project will involve Social Services, schools, Education and other departments sharing information and working together. The project will help councils comply with the information gathering requirements and other standards for looked after children in Quality Protects. An audit tool has been produced by The Who Cares? Trust (1999).

The Equal Chances Project has been developed by The Who Cares? Trust in collaboration with the Calouste Gulbenkian Foundation.

WHERE TO GO FOR HELP

EDUCATION

National Teaching and Advisory Service for Looked After Children and Children in Need
Greenheys Centre, 10 Pencroft Way, Manchester M15 6JJ.
Tel: 0161 232 1001; Fax: 0161 232 1009.
E-mail: NTASLA@aol.com
The National Teaching and Advisory Service provides support packages, recognising the combination of factors involved in the complex difficulties faced by a looked after child. Their case-work model of education builds on an assessment of the children's educational needs in the context of their lives as a whole. A team manager supervises teachers on a monthly basis.

NACRO
169 Clapham Road, London SW9 0PU.
Tel: 020 7582 6500; Fax: 020 7735 0466.
NACRO is a national charity providing a range of services for ex-offenders, those at risk of offending and those who have experienced crime.

Revolving Doors Agency
45-49 Leather Lane, London EC1N 7TJ.
Tel: 020 7242 9222; Fax: 020 7831 5140.
Website: www.revolving-doors.co.uk
The Revolving Doors Agency is a national agency which aims to help people with mental health problems who have been arrested to gain access to support from Health, Social Services and the voluntary sector.

"... her behavioural problems are to be expected in a child with learning disabilities."

> Lucy is eight years old and has a moderate learning disability ('severe learning difficulty in educational terms') owing to Down's syndrome. She can communicate in simple language but is not always easy to understand. Her father died suddenly three years ago and her 55-year-old mother is now terminally ill with cancer. Lucy was a well-adjusted and happy only child making good progress until a few months ago. Since then she has become demanding, clingy, hyperactive, irritable and at times aggressive. Her sleep pattern is poor and she is losing weight. Her special school finds her behaviour difficult to contain at times. Her GP has said that behavioural problems are to be expected in children with learning disabilities.
>
> Lucy has not been told about her mother's illness. Her mother's elder sister may be able to look after Lucy however she is still recovering from a hysterectomy, and is not sure whether she can cope with Lucy's behaviour. Her mother is due to be admitted to a hospice within the next few weeks. Lucy will be in need of a short-term foster family until her aunt has decided whether she can take Lucy on full-time.

This vignette raises the issue of learning disability. The reader is reminded that many young people in care have various problems, which can occur in a number of different combinations.

GENERAL INFORMATION

LEARNING DISABILITY

A child with a learning disability finds it more difficult to learn and understand than other children. Learning disabilities are caused by various factors such as brain injury at birth, brain infection after birth or genetic abnormalities. Examples of conditions often causing severe learning disability include cerebral palsy, Fragile X syndrome and Down's syndrome.

There is frequent confusion caused by the terms that are used to describe children who have a learning disability. The condition used to be known as mental handicap. The Department of Health uses the term 'learning disability', but the Department of Education uses the term 'learning difficulty' (Education Act, 1993). According to the Royal College of Psychiatrists (1998*b*):

the educational category of 'moderate learning difficulties' largely corresponds to the health categories of 'mild' or 'borderline' learning disabilities. It is important to recognise that the need for special educational provision reflects not just a person's cognitive ability but also their social and emotional competence.

About 3 in 1000 children suffer from or show moderate or severe learning disabilities or severe learning difficulties. Within this group approximately 50% suffer from significant psychiatric disorder (Corbett, 1979; Gillberg et al, 1986).

People with learning disabilities almost always need ongoing support throughout their lives. They find learning harder than other people, but that does not mean that they cannot learn. Many people with mild or moderate learning disabilities may go on from school to further education and paid employment. However, people with profound and multiple disabilities need continuous and intensive support.

Key to the good management of children and young people with learning disabilities is effective communication between the families and agencies involved in the child's care and education. It is important to remember that these children are more likely than the general population to suffer from emotional and behavioural disorders. This can be a stressful situation for a child who may have difficulty in expressing themselves and for the adults who are trying to provide the best care and environment for the child. Mental health problems such as behavioural disorders, emotional disorders and self-harm may coexist with each other and should not be considered to be merely a manifestation of learning disability.

QUESTIONS, GUIDANCE AND PROFESSIONAL COMMENT

What support will a child like Lucy need now and in the future?

Lucy is clearly aware that something is going on, but no one seems prepared to talk to her about it. Children with learning disabilities may be intellectually impaired but they are not necessarily emotionally impaired; they are likely to experience the same range of emotions that a non-disabled child would in a similar situation, such as fear, anxiety, distress and upset. There is often the belief that children with disabilities need to be protected from distressing events, and while this is sometimes the case, in Lucy's situation the distressing event is a reality that she cannot be protected from. From Lucy's perspective, something dreadful is happening and she is left trying to guess what it might be. In this situation, one's imagination can run away; she may be thinking that she has done something to cause her mother's illness, that people want to get rid of her, or some other equally painful, but inaccurate thought. This is why it is important to try and talk with Lucy (in line with her age and ability) about what is happening and what is likely to happen. It would be most helpful if someone familiar and consistent to Lucy talked with her, so that she could come back and ask questions or express her feelings when she felt ready.

When the move is imminent, Lucy would benefit from some preparation, however small, such as visiting and meeting the foster family before she actually went to stay with them. Lucy would feel slightly less anxious if she could have familiar and comforting things around her such as photographs, toys and other possessions. It would also be helpful if other aspects of her life were kept consistent wherever possible, such as her daily routines and her school and her after-school activities. These factors should be taken into account if and when she moves in with her aunt.

It is also important that Lucy is given an opportunity to grieve for her mother. This could be facilitated by attending her mother's funeral, placing flowers on her grave, and keeping photographs and personal items of her mother. It is terribly painful when someone you love dies and no amount of protection will remove the pain. If Lucy is given the opportunity and permission to be sad, she will be less likely to communicate her negative feelings in an unhelpful way in the future. It is also important to remember that grief can last several years, that Lucy will lose not only her mother but her home as well and that events such as anniversaries can bring back more intense feelings of loss and grief. Those who work with Lucy in the future should be made aware of her past, so that they can be available to listen, think about and try to understand her feelings.

Dr Sally Hodges

What help can be given to foster families in dealing with behavioural problems from children and adolescents with learning disabilities?

It is true that there is a higher incidence of behavioural problems in children with learning difficulties, but it is not the learning disability that is 'causing' the behavioural difficulty per se. There is also a higher incidence of communication difficulties, and it is more likely that it is this, the child or adolescent's difficulty in communicating their feelings or needs, that is contributing to any behavioural difficulties. It is vital therefore that those working with children with learning disabilities make some effort to open up communication. This can range from making an effort to listen to someone who is unclear in their speech, to using pictures, symbols or signs (like Makaton) to communicate. The aim is to try to think about what the person may be thinking or feeling and to vocalise this. This is the first step in preventing behavioural problems. Where behavioural problems already exist, it is helpful to try and understand from the child's perspective what the key triggers are. This can be done by considering: when it happens (time of day/week); and what it happens in response to (e.g. leaving the home/mealtimes/bedtimes, or when told to do something/when being ignored). This can give clues as to what the behaviour does actually achieve (e.g. more attention/being let off/less attention). It will then be possible to manipulate the situation to reduce or remove the triggers. There are a range of behavioural techniques that can also be helpful, such as rewarding positive behaviours and setting negative consequences for unacceptable behaviour, but these will need to be at a level the child can understand and make sense of.

Dr Sally Hodges

KEY READING

LEARNING DISABILITY

Quinn, P. (1997) *Understanding Disability: A Lifespan Approach*. Thousand Oaks, CA: Sage.

What's going on?

Government programmes and guidance

Quality Protects

This is a major three-year programme which was launched by the Department of Health in November 1998. Quality Protects is about improving the well-being of children in need, which includes those children who are looked after by local authorities (for more information on Quality Protects, see pp. 20–21).

Learning disability

Objective

> To ensure that children with specific social needs arising out of disability or a health condition are living in families or other appropriate settings in the community where their assessed needs are adequately met and reviewed.

A sub-objective of this, which is important, is to arrive at a complete picture of the numbers and circumstances of disabled children by sharing information held by SSDs, Health and Education authorities.

Current research and initiatives

CAMHS Mental Illness Special Grant (MISG)

This grant was first allocated in 1998/1999 to 24 innovative projects (for more information, see p. 21). We have been unable to identify any projects covering the issue of learning disability.

Where to go for help

Learning disability

Disabled Living Foundation
380–384 Harrow Road, London W9 2HU.
Tel: 020 7289 6111; Fax: 020 7266 2922; Helpline: 0870 603 9177; Minicom: 0870 603 9176 (Mon–Fri 10am–4pm).
E-mail: dlfinfo@dlf.org.uk; Website: www.dlf.org.uk
The Disabled Living Foundation is working for freedom, empowerment and choice for disabled people and others who use equipment or technology to enhance their independence. They provide advice and training on equipment for independent living.

Down's Syndrome Association
155 Mitcham Road, London SW17 9PG.
Tel: 020 8682 4001; Fax: 020 8682 4012.
Website: www.downs-syndrome.org.uk
Provides advice and support for all who care for children with Down's syndrome.

The Down Syndrome Educational Trust
The Sarah Duffen Centre, Belmont Street, Southsea, Hampshire PO5 1NA.
Tel: 023 9282 4261; Fax: 023 9282 4265.
E-mail: enquiries@downsnet.org; Website: www.downset.org/
The Down Syndrome Educational Trust exists to advance the development and education of children and adults with Down's syndrome worldwide.

The Family Fund Trust
c/o Joseph Rowntree
PO Box 50, York YO1 9ZX.
Tel: 01904 621115; Textphone: 01904 658085; E-mail: info@familytrustfund.org.uk
Website: www.familytrustfund.org.uk
The Family Fund Trust is funded by the Government to help families with severely disabled children. They are concerned with the child's disability, the family's financial circumstances and the kind of help given.

Mencap
Mencap National Centre, 123 Golden Lane, London EC1Y 0RT.
Tel: 020 7454 0454; Fax: 020 7696 5540.
Website: www.mencap.org.uk
Mencap works with people with learning disabilities to fight discrimination. It campaigns to ensure that their rights are recognised and that they are respected as individuals. It provides residential, education and employment services, leisure opportunities and individual support and advice for people with learning disabilities, their families and carers.

Scope
6 Market Road, London N7 9PW.
Tel: 020 7619 7100; Helpline: 0808 800 3333 (Mon–Fri 9am–9pm, Sat & Sun 2pm–6pm).
E-mail: cphelpline@scope.org.uk
Websites: www.scope.org.uk and www.disabilitynow.org.uk
Provides advice, information and support for those with cerebral palsy or family members of those with cerebral palsy. Topics include: welfare, schools, equipment or anything else to do with living with a disability.

"... she has become very withdrawn and uncommunicative."

Abi is nine and her younger brother Chris is seven. They arrived in England 18 months ago, from Africa. Their mother had sent them to escape the conflict in their country. They could not speak or understand English when they arrived. They were granted refugee status and were placed in a residential home until a suitable foster family could be found. It took a year before a suitable family was found.

Chris has thrived since being moved to the foster family; he has gained weight, is very lively and is behaving like any other boy of his age. The foster family are worried about Abi, who has become very withdrawn and uncommunicative, always appearing miserable and unhappy. Her teacher has spoken to the foster parents, expressing her concerns over Abi's lack of concentration at school, and her inability to bond with her peers.

This vignette raises the issues of refugees and depression in children. The reader is reminded that many young people in care have various problems, which can occur in a number of different combinations. Depression in children can occur for many reasons. Refugee children may suffer no problems at all on arrival in Britain; on the other hand, they may experience a number of problems that may or may not include depression.

GENERAL INFORMATION

DEPRESSION IN CHILDREN

The Health Committee Report (1998) stated that "there is a trend towards a reduction of the average age of children in the care system". The data for year-end 1996 showed that 39% of children in care were under 10 years of age.

It is thought that 2.9% of the general population of children suffer from depression (Kurtz, 1996). For some people, this figure may be unexpected as they do not think of depression as a problem occurring in young children.

We do not have data on the number of young children in care who are suffering from depression. However, we do know that a child in care is more likely to have experienced risk factors which may lead to depression. These may include abuse, violent homes or being removed from the family environment.

Children who have depression are likely to:

- report feeling sad or empty
- appear tearful/irritable
- have a loss of interest and enjoyment
- show reduced energy leading to increased fatigability and diminished activity
- seem very tired after only slight effort.

Other common symptoms include:

- reduced concentration and attention
- reduced self-esteem and self-confidence
- ideas of guilt and unworthiness
- bleak and pessimistic views of the future
- ideas or acts of self-harm or suicide
- disturbed sleep
- diminished appetite (World Health Organization, 1992).

(See also Section 6, which raises the issues of depression in older children and suicide.)

REFUGEES AND UNACCOMPANIED CHILDREN

An 'unaccompanied child or young person' is someone under the age of 18 who is separated from both parents and is not being cared for by an adult who by law or custom has responsibility to do so (United Nations High Commissioner for Refugees, 1994).

Children make up one-half of the world's asylum seekers and refugees, and unaccompanied children make up some 3–5% of the total numbers affected by most large-scale emergencies.

The number of unaccompanied children coming to the UK is increasing:

- In 1992, when the Home Office began keeping records, there were at least 190 applications for asylum.
- In 1997, this figure had risen to 1,105, with 5% of the total applications for asylum being made by unaccompanied children (Ayotte, 1998).
- In 1996, fewer than 2% of children who had a decision made on their asylum applications were recognised as refugees, while 56% were given 'Exceptional Leave to Enter or Remain' (Ayotte, 1998).
- The number of children recognised as refugees in 1997 rose to 27% (Ayotte, 1998).

There are many reasons why children are forced to flee, either alone or with siblings or other children. Often, they flee their own country as a consequence of distressing and frightening events.

However on arrival:

- Most children have had to endure travelling for long periods, often in dangerous situations before arriving in the UK.
- Many unaccompanied children are suffering from: loss, grief, fear and disorientation.
- Many find, owing to complicated legislation, racial discrimination and lack of English language, problems in their social development and educational progress.

QUESTIONS, GUIDANCE AND PROFESSIONAL COMMENT

What approaches are known to be effective in children to treat depression?

Since depression in children often coexists with other psychiatric conditions and with other problems (such as educational failure, impaired psychological functioning, family psycho-pathology, and adverse life events), the management depends on the problems identified during the assessment period. The example of Abi illustrates how children and adolescents displaced as a result of war and political violence have often experienced a number of stressful events, such as loss of home, loss of personal belongings, separation from family members and disruption of schooling and friendships. There may be a marked decline in socio-economic status. Social factors in exile, particularly the level of emotional support, may be important in determining the severity of depressive reactions. Common ongoing stresses may include, as here, separation from family, fears about safety of those left behind and instability of placement.

Research into the effectiveness of different treatments has often been methodologically unsatisfactory. All possible factors contributing to the child's depression should be identified and assessed, and interventions planned appropriately. Despite the strong association between childhood depression and family dysfunction, the few randomised controlled trials of family therapy in childhood depression have not shown any significant differences from comparison interventions. Children under 11 years or so in age are unlikely to be mature enough to undergo cognitive therapy in the same way as adolescents or adults, since there is a need to have the ability to experience negative cognitions, to reflect on these cognitions and to engage in complex reasoning and generate alternative solutions to problems. Further research is required to assess the effectiveness of interpersonal psychotherapy for children with depression. The newer antidepressants, selective serotonin reuptake inhibitors (SSRIs), may have a role to play in treatment. With regard to refugees, there is little research into post-exile factors which may be responsive to change and which may reduce morbidity.

Dr Martin Newman

What are the likely outcomes for children with depression if no help is given?

Most mild and acute cases resolve rapidly; they respond to out-patient treatment and do not recur. For these cases the prognosis is good.

The majority of children with major depression recover within two years. Suicidal thoughts are rare in children, but adolescents with depression are at risk of suicidal behaviour. Little is known about the factors that predict which young person with depression is most at risk of suicidal behaviour, but the risk indicators probably include previous suicide attempts, suicidal thoughts, hopelessness, comorbid problems such as substance misuse and anger, easy access to the method, and lack of social support.

In comparison with children with depression who do not have conduct problems, children who meet criteria for both depressive disorder and conduct disorder seem to have lower rates of depressive disorder when followed into adulthood, but a worse prognosis in terms of substance misuse.

Young people diagnosed as having depression are more likely to have subsequent episodes of depression than those who have not been depressed. One study found that about 70% of child patients with a major depressive disorder had another episode within five years. A similarly high rate of subsequent psychiatric morbidity has been reported in follow-up studies of adolescents with depression that has extended into late adolescence or early adult life. A long-term follow-up by Harrington *et al* (1990) suggested that children and adolescents with depression are four times more likely to have an episode of depression after the age of 17 years than a matched control group.

Little is known about which factors predict the continuity of depression into adulthood. The characteristics of the first episode may be important. Continuity to adulthood is best predicted by a severe adult-like depressive presentation and by the absence of conduct disorder. Older children with depression may have a worse prognosis than younger ones. As with adults, personality problems such as difficulty with forming and sustaining relationships seem to be a poor prognostic feature as far as both treatment and recurrence go. It has been suggested that individuals are changed in one way or another by the first episode of depression, thus becoming more vulnerable to subsequent problems. This suggests that much greater attention should be paid to the recognition and treatment of the first episode of depression.

Dr Martin Newman

Will a child's refugee status influence the effectiveness of the care approach?

Wherever they may be placed, these children and young people have to struggle in order to adjust to a whole new way of life, from the country's climate to every level of human interaction. They have to learn a new language and new social norms and expectations. They are also forced to deal with officials and organisations whose existence, let alone function, is alien to them. The concept and the experience of being alone (psychologically) are daunting for these children. While some may view this as an opportunity for a new beginning, for the majority it is only the beginning of a new life without all that was familiar and safe. Overnight, they have lost any clear boundaries; the secure, consistent care and support from trusted family members, as well as from close friends and neighbours. They are frightened, confused, disorientated by the new way of life and daunted by what may lie ahead.

Despite their individual differences these are uprooted children and they all need support at close hand. Grinberg & Grinberg (1989) describe uprooted children as 'unsettled' – children who, they add, "exhibit maladjustment, manifest phobias, retreat into isolation, reject school, inhibit [their] own abilities and have learning problems". For African children, dealing with racism in a new society compounds the difficulties that refugees are having to face regardless of their race. Although it may be difficult to know at what point uprooted children become psychologically affected, it appears that the uncertainty of their position in the new society plays a significant part in triggering some of the difficulties they present. The adults caring for or providing support to these children need to understand the children's experiences and their context, in order to provide appropriate support for these vulnerable children.

If the support these children receive is not sensitive and appropriate, it can be detrimental to their healing and recovery process, thus affecting their development in the long term. Observations indicate that the younger the children, the easier it is for them to overcome their difficult experiences. They appear to find it easier to integrate into the new society, over a shorter period of time. They often respond well to the support and care provided by substitute carers in the receiving country.

These young people need to feel trusted. Yet, often secrecy is imposed to protect their families and the children are therefore perceived as being emotionally reserved. They are criticised for being 'quiet', 'secretive', 'withdrawn', 'hostile' and generally 'choosing not to communicate'. They should not be held responsible and subsequently punished for a way of life which has been imposed on them. They are subjected to further harassment, often as a result of the helping professionals not understanding their context sufficiently. Those providing support and care for these children must be aware of the assumptions and prejudices they themselves hold and operate with.

With older children, however, the memories are likely to be more vivid and the loss felt more acutely. Older children may also have 'guilts' and 'secrets'. They fear persecution from new authorities, however well-meaning they might be. This remains part of their ongoing reality; they continue to perceive themselves to be protecting those loved ones they have left behind. These young people are unfortunately criticised and accused of telling lies and for not being honest about their background.

People and groups like asylum seekers/refugees are categorised on many levels. In terms of status, those with refugee status are better regarded and have a better status than those who are still waiting for decisions. Refugees have better benefits. They are therefore more likely to feel settled and able to access services and to look forward to planning for their future. Those awaiting decisions are left in limbo, uncertain of their future, caught up in the constant anxiety phase. They are faced with the fear of possible moves and further losses. As one young interviewee explained "You can't live properly, it's always on your mind, you might be asked to leave". Another person added, "It is like being a prisoner in your mind but not your body."

Some children have found that being in care impacts on their role as older siblings. In some situations, they feel they are losing their status, where they would have had a role as the substitute carer to the younger sibling. This loss of the real or perceived role can trigger feelings of loss again and of not being needed. Without this role, they feel they have lost the only way to normalise this world again. They often use these relationships as a way of holding on to all the attachments and values they had before the disruptions in exile.

Some behaviours that might be characterised as positive in one culture are seen as negative in other cultures. In the new environment, these young people may experience rejection, and this makes them not only question their self-image, but also the whole context they lived in before – their upbringing, their relationships, etc. This in turn could lead them to reject their roots, while attempting to belong and to become an accepted member in the new society. Outside of their own environment, where they counted for someone and somebody, the children are now seen as outsiders. Because of the negative images, they gradually lose the significant features which they held for themselves and others in their own society.

Having to accept the undesirable status of their existence is an ongoing and painful experience, which gradually distorts their perception of the world and may drive them to antisocial and other difficult behaviours. The more they experience rejection, the more negative the impact on their psychological well-being.

Refugee status, once achieved, does not remove children's anxiety about their future. The guilt of their being safe and not their loved ones can continue to make them feel sad, helpless and angry. They may continue experiencing difficulties in adapting to their new lives and living with the separation. For some, gaining recognition as refugees eases their fear of deportation and allows them to feel safe and no longer in limbo. They may begin to feel legitimate and more accepted as part of the new context.

Engaging with individual children should be viewed as a developmental process. This involves progression through ongoing successive stages of transitions. They may well reject their own roots initially, to belong. They will, however, come round in their own time to appreciate and

Box 4. Strategies for supporting refugee children

- **Listen to the child**. It is important to hear what children are saying and not only what you want to hear.
- **Ask – do not assume**. Each individual has their own unique experiences and social/cultural context.
- **Pace your approach accordingly**. Avoid temptation to find out everything because it is needed for assessment work. (Some things can wait – have you checked?)
- **Consider language barriers**. Use interpreters. The initial open communication is crucial to the success of the relationship. It is important to check with the young people first. They need to be allowed some choice, because different social and political groups may have difficulties relating.
- **Be clear of your role**. Explain the differences between the different professional groups and why the children might come into contact with them.
- **Keep the line of communication open and frequent**. This helps in building trust and continuity.
- **Share**. Let them experience the new context through yourself. Norms of different societies, as well as similarities and differences within a new and past context, can be shared without having to include personal issues.
- **Encourage support**. Allow anyone they identify as a friend or support to accompany them and to join your discussions if they should choose to do so.
- **Whatever the circumstances, show respect**. As the young people have lost a great deal, this gives them back some sense of self-worth and motivation to succeed in the new context. Giving information on plans for them, keeping appointments, etc. are important to the young people as a measure of respect from others in a place of authority.

respect their background; their language, their history and all the different aspects of their rich culture. Professionals have a duty to break such barriers to reach these vulnerable children and young people. Each individual has a story to tell – a unique story – and they deserve to be heard and assessed within a culturally sensitive and appropriate framework.

In a recent interview, a number of young people from Africa stated that their main reasons for their difficulty in settling were directly related to the language barrier, not understanding the different concepts of the care system and their general fear of the unknown. They also commented that carers and staff in residential homes do not always understand them. For them, the best way to cope with communication difficulties is often to keep quiet. Some added that expressing their views or feelings often made no difference; their solution, therefore, was to keep quiet and let things sort themselves out.

The final point that needs to be made is one which concerns the working theory of the professional. As professionals working with people from diverse backgrounds, we need to question our own assumptions, on which we have based our research and knowledge. Do we question to what extent the existing knowledge can be generalised to people from other cultural backgrounds?

There are limitations to working with only existing theories. All professionals have an obligation and responsibility to carry out their work from a culturally sensitive knowledge base. Therefore, we owe it to the young people we support to approach each individual with an open mind and willingness to learn about cultural backgrounds different from our own. Existing traditional viewpoints should be reviewed in the light of a cross-cultural perspective.

We need more research with a substantial cross-cultural knowledge base. Using the strategies in Box 4 will assist professionals and carers to maximise conditions for the appropriate assessment and support of refugee children and young people.

Mrs Matesebia Tadesse

KEY READING

DEPRESSION

American Academy of Child and Adolescent Psychiatry (1998) Practice parameters for the assessment and treatment of children and adolescents with depressive disorders. *Journal of the American Academy of Child and Adolescent Psychiatry*, **37** (suppl. 10).

Goodyer, I. (ed.) (1995) *The Depressed Child and Adolescent. Developmental and Clinical Perspectives*. Cambridge: Cambridge University Press.

Graham, P. & Hughes, C. (1997) *So Young, So Sad, So Listen*. London: Gaskell/ West London Health Promotion Agency.

Harrington, R., Whittaker, J., Shoebridge, P., *et al* (1998). Systematic review of efficacy of cognitive behaviour therapies in child and adolescent depressive disorder. *British Medical Journal*, **316**, 1559–1563.

REFUGEE CHILDREN

Ayotte, W. (1998) *Supporting Unaccompanied Children in the Asylum Process*. London: Save the Children.

What's going on?

Government programmes and guidance

Quality Protects and National Priorities Guidance

These documents do not refer to the issues of depression or refugee children (for more information on these Government initiatives see pp. 20–21).

Current research and initiatives

CAMHS Mental Illness Specific Grant (MISG)

These documents do not refer to the issues of depression or refugee children (for more information on these Government initiatives see p. 21). We have been unable to identify any relevant projects on these issues.

Other regional studies

Refugee children

Children of the Storm (COTS), 61 Oak Grove, Cricklewood, London NW2 3LS.
Tel: 020 8450 0223.

To assist young refugees in adjusting to life in the UK, a group of young people and teachers created the above charity. COTS was established to cater for the emotional and material needs of the increasing number of young asylum seekers entering Britain.

COTS supports refugees under the age of 21, directly and indirectly by:

- raising awareness through producing information material;
- providing financial assistance – COTS runs a small grants scheme to provide emergency financial support to refugee children;
- through the 'Schools Link' project, promoting peer support groups and giving presentations and advice to schools and community groups on how to increase their capacity to integrate refugees and give them support; and
- running study support schemes which assist refugees with learning English and doing homework.

Where to go for help

General

Careline
Tel: 020 8514 1177 (Mon–Fri 10am–4pm, 7pm–10pm).
Confidential counselling for young people and adults. Can also refer callers to other organisations and support groups throughout the country.

ChildLine
Freepost 1111, London N1 OBR.
Tel: 0800 1111 (24 hours).
Provides confidential counselling, support and advice on any issue.

ChildLine for Children in Care
Freepost 1111, Glasgow G1 1BR.
Tel: 0800 884444.
A special free telephone number for children and young people who are looked after. Provides confidential counselling, support and advice on any issue.

MIND Infoline
Granta House, 15–19 Broadway, Stratford, London E15 4BQ.
Tel: 020 8522 1728 or 08457 660163 (outside London); Helpline: 0345 660133.
Provides information on all aspects of mental health.

The Samaritans
10 The Grove, Slough, Berkshire SL1 1QP.
Tel: 01753 532713; Fax: 01753 775787; Helpline: 0345 909090 (24 hours);
E-mail: jo@samaritans.org; Website: www.samaritans.org.uk
Offers free emotional support to anyone going through difficulties.

Voice for the Child in Care
Unit 4, Pride Court, 80–82 White Lion Street, London N1 9PF.
Tel: 020 7833 5792; Freephone (for young people only): 0808 8005792.
This service offers advocacy (a voice) for children and young people in or leaving care.

Who Cares? LinkLine
Tel: 020 7251 3117; Helpline: 0500 56 45 70 (Mon, Wed & Thurs 3.30pm–6.30pm).
Offers information and support to young people who are or who have been in care.

YoungMinds Parents Information Service
2nd Floor, 102–108 Clerkenwell Road, London EC1M 5SA.
Tel: 020 7336 8445; Fax: 020 7336 8446; Helpline: 0345 626376.
This service is for parents or carers with concerns about the mental health or emotional well-being of a child or young person. Provides information and details of local and national services.

Youth Access
2 Taylors Yard, 67 Alderbrook Road, London SW12 8AD.
Tel: 020 8772 9900; Fax: 020 8772 9746; E-mail: yaccess@dircon.co.uk
Youth Access can give details and information of counselling services in the child or young person's local area.

Refugees and asylum seekers

Amnesty International
99–119 Rosebury Avenue, London EC1R 4RE.
Tel: 020 7814 6200; Fax: 020 7833 1510; E-mail: information@amnesty.org.uk
Website: www.amnesty.org.uk
Provides information and resources on global human rights issues.

Refugee Council
3 Bondway, London SW8 1SJ.
Tel: 020 7820 3085; Fax: 020 7582 9929.
E-mail: refcounciluk@gn.apc.org; Website: www.refugeecouncil.org.uk
Resources, support and advice for refugees and asylum seekers and those supporting them.

Refugee Support Centre
47 South Lambeth Road, London SW8 1RH.
Tel: 020 7820 3606.
The Refugee Support Centre offers a free and confidential therapeutic service to refugees and asylum seekers who are experiencing emotional or psychological distress.

Save the Children
17 Grove Lane, London SE5 8RD.
Tel: 020 7703 5400.
Website: www.savethechildren.org.uk
Save the Children supports young refugees and asylum seekers in various projects around the world.

United Nations High Commission for Refugees (UNHCR)
21st Floor, Millbank Tower, 21–24 Millbank, London SW1P 4QP.
Tel: 020 7828 9191.
UNHCR promotes public awareness of refugee issues and coordinates humanitarian aid to some refugee populations.

World University Service
14 Dufferin Street, London EC1Y 8PD.
Tel: 020 7426 5820; Fax: 020 7251 1315.
This service campaigns on educational issues throughout the world and runs an educational advice service for asylum seekers and refugees who wish to enrol at further and higher educational institutes.

"... his social worker is concerned that this extra stress may push him over the edge."

John is 15. He has been in care since the age of 12. John was born when his mother was 18. She met her new partner when John was 10. She soon became pregnant and her partner did not want John around. John went to live with his natural father. His father had become increasingly dependent on cannabis and also drank heavily. He found working and looking after his son very difficult. It wasn't long before John was left alone, a lot of the time, while his father went out drinking or visiting friends. This was reported to Social Services and John was taken into care. Originally, this was only a temporary measure, as Social Services tried to re-unite John with his mother. However, this reconciliation has recently broken down completely, and John remains in residential care.

His social worker is extremely worried about him. Over the past three months, John has stopped his involvement in a number of leisure activities that he once enjoyed, including the school's football team and computer club. He also appears to be losing weight, and shows no interest in food. His teacher has been in contact with the residential home, as she has noticed a lack of concentration from him in his classes and says he is becoming increasingly uncooperative. His GCSEs are coming up in a couple of month's time and his social worker is concerned that this extra stress may push him over the edge.

This vignette raises the issues of teenage depression, suicide and parental substance misuse. The reader is reminded that many young people in care have various problems, which can occur in a number of different combinations. Each of the issues raised, whether individually or in combination with other issues, could equally cause problems for a young person.

GENERAL INFORMATION

A young person with depression experiences profound unhappiness and a sense of dejection that is beyond normal sadness. Although the term 'depression' is often used to describe a frequent human emotion, it can also refer to a psychiatric disorder. Young people with depression feel miserable and unhappy. They may be negative in their approach and seem to have lost interest in things around them. They may lose weight, change their sleeping pattern, experience a loss of energy, have feelings of guilt or self-blame, or feel that their situation is hopeless and have recurring thoughts of death or suicide. In a study of 32 adolescents in the care system who were referred to a direct access child mental health service in the UK, Butler & Vostanis (1998) found that 50% of the adolescents had features of a depressive disorder. McCann *et al* (1996), in their study examining the prevalence of psychiatric disorders in adolescents in the care system in Oxfordshire, found 23% suffering from a major depressive disorder, compared with 4% of adolescents in their control group. The prevalence of depression in the general population is thought to be 1.0%–4.2% for adolescents (Kurtz, 1996).

(See also Section 5, which raises the issue of depression in young children.)

SUICIDE

By the mid-1980s in Britain and in almost all European countries, as well as the USA, suicide among young people was markedly greater than any other decade. In many parts of the world, it had become the second most frequent cause of death, after accident, among the 15–24-year-old age group (NHS Health Advisory Service, 1994).

Male suicide rates in the 15–24 age group increased from just under 10 per 100,000 population to approximately 16 per 100,000 between the years 1976–81 and 1986–91; a 60% increase (NHS Health Advisory Service, 1994). The figures for young women show no change at all, with the rate remaining at just under 5 per 100,000. Therefore, it would seem that young males are three times more likely to commit suicide than young women.

PARENTAL SUBSTANCE MISUSE

The term 'substance' covers legal and illegal drugs and over-the-counter and prescribed medication. 'Drug use', 'misuse' and 'abuse' are often used interchangeably and have a range of meanings including experimental, recreational, socially unacceptable and excessive use of drugs. Here 'substance misuse' is used to mean problematic use of any substance (see above) – defined as causing damage to physical or mental health and often having adverse effects on the drug user's family, the community and society in general. However, it is important to remember that any drug use has the potential to impede parents' ability to care for their child. Drug problems can affect people's lives in very different ways and the effects depend on various factors including the individual, their psychological and physical state, the drugs used and the quantity and methods of use. Other factors include the situations in which drugs are used, whether drugs are used in combination with others such as alcohol, whether drug use is away from children and whether the adults who are not intoxicated are present.

QUESTIONS, GUIDANCE AND PROFESSIONAL COMMENT

How does depression differ from 'normal' moody teenage behaviour?

Mild doubts about the purpose of life are not uncommon among intelligent adolescents. Downward mood swings are quite common in adolescents, particularly girls, although they are not usually severe. Depressive symptoms (such as sad mood, misery and tearfulness) are common in emotionally disturbed children and adolescents, and are most likely to be found in children with unfortunate life experiences. It may be clear that the unhappiness is a proportionate and potentially reversible response to circumstances. Overdoses are taken for various reasons, not necessarily because the adolescent is suffering from a depressive illness.

The clinical picture of depression in adolescents is usually comparable with that in early-adult life, with low mood, tiredness, inappropriate guilt, self-deprecation, sleep difficulties, anxiety, suicidal thoughts, and other symptoms. Social withdrawal and anhedonia are powerful indicators of the presence of depression. Not all symptoms may be present in any one case. The presenting problem may be running away from home, separation anxiety (which may present as school refusal), hypochondrias, antisocial behaviour (in boys), a decline in school work, a change (increase or decrease) in appetite, weight loss (possibly masked by continuing growth), complaints of 'boredom', poor memory, poor concentration and substance misuse. An important feature of depressive disorders in childhood and adolescence is the frequency of comorbidity.

Information needs to be collected from several sources, including the young person themselves, since parents and teachers may under-estimate the severity of the adolescent's feelings. There are a number of questionnaires, standardised interviews and other measures which may be helpful – some for identifying the presence of depression and others for measurement of change during treatment.

Dr Martin Newman

Looking after children or young people who are severely depressed is a stressful experience for support workers and foster parents and their families. It is always advisable to seek help if you are concerned about the well-being of a child in your care. In the short term, the advice in Box 5 may be of help.

What approach(es) are known to be the most effective in treating severe depression in an adolescent?

Box 5. Strategies for helping children/adolescents with depression

- Listen to the child.
- Notice and promote the positive and hopeful aspects of what they say and do.
- Praise them for letting you know they are sad and for not trying to deal with it on their own.
- Let them know that you are sensitive to their sadness but that you can bear it (and them) and retain hope.
- Don't get into a role of making them cheer up.
- Don't dismiss their feelings.

Dr Margaret Hunter

A child or adolescent who is expressing suicidal thoughts should be referred, as an urgent case, to a child and adolescent mental health service (CAMHS). Children or adolescents with depression require a psychiatric assessment. Coexisting psychiatric conditions, educational difficulties, impaired psychosocial functioning, family psychopathology, and adverse life events are all issues that need to be addressed.

Management depends upon the severity of the depression. Selective serotonin reuptake inhibitors (SSRIs) are increasingly used because of early indications that they are effective, unlike tricyclic antidepressants, which have not been shown to work. SSRIs should be considered for children and adolescents who have psychotic depression or bipolar depression; those who are not responding to an adequate trial of psychotherapy. They should also be considered for children or young people whose symptoms are interfering with academic and social functioning or are impeding an adequate trial of psychotherapy, and for those with recurrent depressions that do not respond to or cannot be prevented with psychotherapy. Adult doses of antidepressants are often required in order to achieve sufficient blood levels in teenagers. SSRIs are relatively safe in overdose but carry a risk of precipitating excitable or agitated behaviour. The response to antidepressants may not occur before 8–12 weeks and is commonly out of phase with parents' or carers' observations; they detect improvement before the child reports it, but the child (or, especially, adolescent) may then claim cure while parents or carers have reservations.

With regard to other therapeutic approaches, adolescents with severe depression are less likely to respond to cognitive–behavioural therapies than those with moderate depression. Interpersonal psychotherapy may be of help to adolescents with moderate depression. Further research is needed to determine when to use psychological treatments, when to use medication, and whether combining the two confers any additional advantages.

Dr Martin Newman

What is best practice in looking after a child or adolescent whom a professional believes may attempt suicide?

Always listen to the child. Children and adolescents who have serious suicidal intentions always require a psychiatric assessment and may require counselling or medical treatment in some form.

The first step when caring for a child or young person such as John is to assess the perceived risk of them actually attempting suicide. Many teenagers in conflict or who are severely depressed have a risk of taking an overdose, but few however make serious plans to kill themselves. If it is felt that they really do intend to attempt to kill themselves, they should be urgently assessed by their local CAMHS.

Although extremely serious attempts at suicide are often pre-meditated, reducing the likelihood of impulsive acts is partly helpful. This means securing and identifying all items that could be used to inflict harm, such as medications and razors.

Dr Stephen Kingsbury

What effect can substance misuse by parents have on their children?

Most parents who use drugs are 'good enough' parents and do not neglect or abuse their children (Local Government Drugs Forum & Standing Conference on Drug Abuse, 1997).

Indeed, most parents who use drugs, including alcohol, will not neglect or harm their children. A number of British and American studies have reported a high correlation between parental drug misuse and child protection concerns, although writers are quick to point out that on its own, drug use must not be seen as an indicator of abuse or neglect. There is a need to establish in what way, if any, the drug use is putting the child at risk (Mounteney, 1998).

In circumstances where problematic drug use is taking place, parents may prevent children from receiving the care that they need and that their parents would like them to receive. The lifestyle of drug misusing parents can be unstable. They may be experiencing financial difficulties, problems with the criminal justice system and stays in hospital.

The risk factors for child physical and mental health include:

- risks associated with the mental state and behaviour of the parent which can lead to a lack of parental awareness of the needs of the child and the need to seek external support;
- risks in the social environment – for example, contact with other drug-using peers;
- risks in the physical environment including leaving drugs around the home;
- poor bonding skills;
- poor parenting skills; and
- uncontrolled drug use.

In cases where parents are regularly 'intoxicated' a child may become 'over-responsible', taking on the duties that are normally carried out by their parents.

A NHS Health Advisory Service review (1996) indicated that children of drug-using parents may be at greater risk of developing substance misuse problems later in life than the children of parents who do not use drugs. More evidence is being gathered about the effect of problem drug users on children's emotional development.

On the whole, however, commentators agree that the weight of evidence shows that parenting skills and family life are likely to deteriorate when parents misuse drugs. The psychological risks to children of drug-using parents are reasonably well established, with CAMHS reporting that longstanding drug or alcohol misuse by a parent is a statistical risk factor for child and adolescent mental health.

The effect of parental drug misuse on the emotional and psychological development of the child is of great concern. Drug-using parents' child-raising behaviour may be characterised by lack of consistency and unreliability. They may also be undependable and exhibit un-predictable behaviour. There is also an increased risk, in extreme cases, of violence, both physical and sexual, towards the child.

Parental drug misuse can result in the child feeling guilty or even responsible for their parents' behaviour. The child's role in concealing the family's drug misuse may result in isolation and loneliness, for example as a result of lack of contact with friends within their home environment in case their secret is revealed. They can also experience trauma resulting from the parents' mood swings and often unpredictable behaviour. Other psychological and emotional strain is also encountered because of the child's fear of parental separation and/or the absence of their parent(s).

The child's psychological trauma may manifest itself in anxiety, sadness and depression, restlessness and loss of concentration, mood swings and aggression, low self-esteem, poor school performance and truancy. In general, the child's emotional and psychological development may be hindered. However, the extent of impact of parental harm on the child can be dependent on other factors, such as style and quality of relationships within the family.

Ms Joanne Butcher

KEY READING

DEPRESSION AND SUICIDE

American Academy of Child and Adolescent Psychiatry (1998) Practice parameters for the assessment and treatment of children and adolescents with depressive disorders. *Journal of the American Academy of Child and Adolescent Psychiatry*, **37** (suppl. 10).

Harrington, R., Whittaker, J. & Shoebridge, P. (1998) Psychological treatment of depression in children and adolescents: a review of treatment research. *British Journal of Psychiatry*, **173**, 291–298.

Hazell, P., O'Connell, D., Heathcote, D., *et al* (1995) Efficacy of tricyclic drugs in treating child and adolescent depression: a meta-analysis. *British Medical Journal*, **310**, 897–901.

WHAT'S GOING ON?

GOVERNMENT PROGRAMMES AND GUIDANCE

Quality Protects and National Priorities Guidance

These documents do not refer to the issues of depression or parental substance misuse (for more information on these Government initiatives, see pp. 20–21).

CURRENT RESEARCH AND INITIATIVES

CAMHS Mental Illness Specific Grant (MISG)

This grant was first allocated in 1998/1999 to 24 innovative projects (for more information, see p. 21). We have been unable to identify any projects relevant to these issues.

WHERE TO GO FOR HELP

GENERAL

Careline
Tel: 020 8514 1177 (Mon–Fri 10am–4pm, 7pm–10pm).
Confidential counselling for young people and adults. Can also refer callers to other organisations and support groups throughout the country.

ChildLine
Freepost 1111, London N1 OBR.
Tel: 0800 1111 (24 hours).
Provides confidential counselling, support and advice on any issue.

ChildLine for Children in Care
Freepost 1111, Glasgow G1 1BR.
Tel: 0800 884444.
A special free telephone number for children and young people who are looked after. Provides confidential counselling, support and advice on any issue.

Manic Depression Fellowship
8–10 High Street, Kingston Upon Thames, Surrey KT1 1EY.
Tel: 020 8974 6550; Fax: 020 8974 6600.
This organisation gives support, help and advice to people with manic depression, their relatives and friends. It aims to remove the stigma of mental illness and improve knowledge and understanding among the public and professionals.

MIND Infoline
Granta House, 15–19 Broadway, Stratford, London E15 4BQ.
Tel: 020 8522 1728 or 08457 660163 (outside London).
Provides information on all aspects of mental health.

The Samaritans
10 The Grove, Slough, Berkshire SL1 1QP.
Tel: 01753 532713; Fax: 01753 775787; Helpline: 0345 909090 (24 hours);
E-mail: jo@samaritans.org; Website: www.samaritans.org.uk
Offers free emotional support to anyone going through difficulties.

Voice for the Child in Care
Unit 4, Pride Court, 80–82 White Lion Street, London N1 9PF.
Tel: 020 7833 5792; Freephone (for young people only): 0808 8005792.
This service offers advocacy (a voice) for children and young people in or leaving care.

Who Cares? LinkLine
Tel: 020 7251 3117; Fax: 020 7251 3123; Helpline: 0500 56 45 70 (Mon, Wed & Thurs 3.30pm–6.30pm).
Offers information and support to young people who are or who have been in care.

YoungMinds Parents Information Service
2nd Floor, 102–108 Clerkenwell Road, London EC1M 5SA.
Tel: 020 7336 8445; Fax: 020 7336 8446; Helpline: 0345 626376.

"... last night he spoke of the television telling him that people were watching him."

Mark is 14. He was taken into care at the age of nine after his father was sentenced to eight years in prison for armed robbery. His stepmother was unable to cope with five young children. For the past five years, Mark and his younger sister Louise have been living with their long-term foster family. They settled in very quickly with their new family, which also includes Tom, an older brother for them both.

Mark's foster parents became concerned about him a few months ago, when his interest in his school work began to diminish and he started spending a lot of time alone. They originally presumed it was just 'his age'. However in the past few weeks, Mark has begun to appear totally absorbed within himself and very uncommunicative. His foster parents, on a couple of occasions, have found his speech difficult to follow.

Mark's foster mother is now extremely concerned for him. Last night he told her that the television was telling him that "people were watching him". This morning he told his foster brother to get off the telephone, as "they were listening". He became very distressed and upset as Tom ignored his comments and remained on the telephone.

This vignette raises the issue of psychotic disorders. The reader is reminded that many young people in care have various problems, which can occur in a number of different combinations.

GENERAL INFORMATION

PSYCHOTIC DISORDERS

Psychotic disorders are a severe form of mental illness. Early diagnosis and medical treatment are important. The two most common types of psychotic disorder or 'psychoses' are schizophrenia and bipolar disorder. Psychotic disorders are rare in childhood and adolescence. Schizophrenia affects approximately 1 in 100 people at some time in their lives; it is very unusual for it to start before the age of 15 but then the rate increases rapidly with age. Bipolar disorder is also extremely rare before the age of 15. A study of children in the local care system in Oxford (McCann *et al*, 1996) found that 8% of the children and young people had a psychotic condition. This is well above the numbers we would expect to find in the general population.

Schizophrenia usually begins when a person is between 15 and 35 years of age. It affects a young person's thoughts, emotions and behaviour. The illness often persists for a long time and can be very disabling. Schizophrenia tends to run in families. A child who has an affected parent has a 1 in 10 chance of developing schizophrenia. Evidence from research suggests that stressful events, or difficult relationships in the family, can sometimes trigger an episode of schizophrenia.

Children or young people who have schizophrenia may behave differently from adults who have this condition. Early warning signs may include:

- confused thinking
- trouble telling dreams from reality
- vivid and strange thoughts and ideas
- extreme moodiness
- strange behaviours
- behaving like a younger child
- refusing to speak
- severe anxiety and fearfulness
- seeing things and hearing voices which are not real
- confusing television with reality
- thinking that people are 'out to get them'.

Children and young people with **bipolar affective disorder** show extreme changes in mood. They have periods of being very 'high' or manic, and very 'low' or depressed. Sometimes people refer to this condition as manic–depressive disorder. Bipolar affective disorder is very rare before puberty. The causes are not fully understood, but it is thought to run in families and can be triggered by a physical illness or, like schizophrenia, by stressful events. Young people with bipolar affective disorder may show a number of the signs listed below:

- depression, moodiness, irritability, excitement or elation
- very rapid speech and changes of subject
- loss of energy or excessive energy
- loss of appetite and weight
- sleep disturbances
- neglect of personal care
- withdrawal from friends, or excessive sociability
- feelings of guilt, hopelessness or worthlessness
- inflated ideas about themselves or their abilities
- reckless behaviour, excessive spending or sexual promiscuity.

It should be noted that drug usage may mimic psychotic states.

Young people with severe mental illness may need to be admitted to an in-patient unit for a significant period of time. It is very important for the young person that their carer or foster parent remains closely involved in their management (Hunter, 1993).

Questions, guidance and professional comment

Is diagnosing a young person with a psychiatric disorder just a way of labelling or 'medicalising' the young person's difficulties?

Frequently, professionals from social services express concern about the limitations of diagnosing psychiatric disorders in young people and perceive this as labelling or medicalising the young person's difficulties.

Young people often experience a sense of relief when they have a label or a diagnosis for their difficulties as they then have clearer access to resources. However, diagnosing a young person with a psychiatric disorder also has its disadvantages in that a great deal of their behaviour is then put down to the psychiatric disorder and it is hard for the young person and the family to separate that from ordinary growing-up problems. Inevitably, young people with psychiatric labels are stigmatised by their own peer group and often by society at large.

The question that has to be asked is in whose interest and benefit is it that a psychiatric label is given. Just as a psychiatric label can give access to professional resources, it can also give access to resources within the self-help community for young people experiencing psychiatric problems. This is a domain of expertise that is often ignored by professionals. Young people, in my experience, are extremely willing to share with each other the strategies they have for coping with their psychiatric disorder.

How, though, do we then also see young people with a psychiatric disorder as young people who have many competencies and resources of their own, rather than seeing them as just people with a disability? For example, how do their friends understand this disorder, what allowances do their friends make and how do their friends still have good expectations of them? How can the young person's own experience and expertise of living with their disorder be best used rather than marginalised?

Children such as Mark suffering from a psychotic disorder, clearly need a referral to a specialist child and adolescent mental health team. These children, in particular, need a prompt assessment and diagnoses so that appropriate management can begin as soon as possible. This is not a condition that can be left untreated. Children and young people with schizophrenia require specialist treatment and this can only be instigated after a thorough assessment (to rule out other possible causes of the behaviour) and a diagnosis has been made.

Ms Carol Halliwell

What does research suggest is the best treatment for a young person suffering from psychotic illness?

A holistic approach to treatment for a young person such as Mark is essential and should include the following components:

- **Antipsychotic medication** to stabilise acute symptoms: ideally, one of the new or 'atypical' antipsychotic drugs will be used, since they are less likely to cause distressing side-effects.
- **Psychoeducation** for both the young person and their parents/carers designed to increase their understanding of the nature of psychotic illness and the increased vulnerability to stress accompanying it.

- **Psychosocial intervention** with the young person and parents/carers designed to decrease the level of any expressed emotion, e.g. critical comments, over-intrusiveness and other factors that may increase the level of stress in the household.
- **Cognitive–behavioural therapy** designed to help the young person recognise warning signs of relapse, develop strategies to minimise the risk of relapse and also strategies to cope with residual symptoms, such as hearing voices.
- **Comprehensive rehabilitation** services designed to help the young person return to education or employment and resume age-appropriate social relationships.

Dr David Will

What are the likely outcomes if a child or adolescent receives no help for their illness?

If the psychotic illness is schizophrenia, without treatment the vast majority of children and adolescents remain unwell and their condition is likely to deteriorate. In the short term, they will continue to suffer from symptoms such as hallucinations and delusions and are likely to become progressively more withdrawn or to exhibit more bizarre behaviour. In the longer term, there is evidence which suggests that the outcome of schizophrenia is significantly worse in people who are not treated within the first year of its onset. Such people may become progressively more lethargic and lacking in motivation, their life in essence having come to a halt. It is therefore vitally important that schizophrenia is treated as early as possible.

If the psychotic illness is bipolar affective disorder (also known as manic depression) the young person, if untreated, is likely to be subject to episodes of extreme swings in mood.

Dr David Will

KEY READING

PSYCHOTIC DISORDERS

American Academy of Child and Adolescent Psychiatry (1994) Practice parameters for the assessment of children and adolescents with schizophrenia. *Journal of American Academy of Child and Adolescent Psychiatry*, **33**, 616–635.

American Academy of Child and Adolescent Psychiatry (1997) Practice parameters for the assessment and treatment of children and adolescents with bipolar disorder. *American Academy of Child and Adolescent Psychiatry*, **36** (suppl. 10).

WHAT'S GOING ON?

GOVERNMENT PROGRAMMES AND GUIDANCE

Quality Protects and National Priorities Guidance

These documents do not refer to the issues of psychosis (for more information on these Government initiatives, see pp. 20–21).

CURRENT RESEARCH AND INITIATIVES

CAMHS Mental Illness Specific Grant (MISG)

This grant was first allocated in 1998/1999 to 24 innovative projects (for more information, see p. 21). We have been unable to identify any projects covering this issue.

WHERE TO GO FOR HELP

PSYCHOTIC DISORDERS

Sane
Ist Floor, Cityside House, 40 Adler Street, London E1 1EE.
Tel: 020 7375 1002; Saneline: 0345 67 80 00 (all week 2pm–midnight).
Provides information and support to people suffering from mental illness, their friends and family.

Manic Depression Fellowship
8–10 High Street, Kingston Upon Thames, Surrey KT1 1EY.
Tel: 020 8974 6550.
Gives support, help and advice to people with manic depression, their relatives and friends. It aims to remove the stigma of mental illness and improve knowledge and understanding among professionals and the public.

National Schizophrenia Fellowship
25 Castle Street, Kingston Upon Thames, Surrey KT1 1SS.
Tel: 020 8547 3937.
Website: www.nsf.org.uk
A national voluntary organisation that helps people with a severe mental illness, their families and carers. The Foundation's particular concern is with schizophrenia and related conditions.

"... she got involved in prostitution to help pay for her drug habit."

Claire is 14 years old. She has been in care for 18 months. Claire's problems started at a very young age. Her parents were heavy drinkers and they would often abuse Claire and her younger sisters physically and emotionally. When Claire's mother was drunk, she would hit and insult Claire or lock her in her bedroom, only allowing her out to clean the house or cook meals. These family experiences led to Claire missing a lot of school. When she was at school, she would often play truant, as she felt that being so behind with the work there was no point in attending classes.

She began smoking cannabis and drinking heavily at the age of 11 and began experimenting with other drugs from 12 onwards. Eventually, Claire had had enough of her home life and ran away. She lived on the streets and got involved with prostitution to help pay for her drug habit. Claire was picked up by the police, who subsequently reported her to Social Services.

She has been living in a residential home since then, although she often goes missing from the home. The police have picked her up three times in the past month for prostitution. Claire has just found out that she is three months pregnant from her 'boyfriend', who is a well-known drug dealer in the area. She has decided that she would like to keep the baby, and needs help to come off 'crack'.

This vignette raises the issues of substance misuse, physical and emotional abuse and teenage pregnancy. The reader is reminded that many young people in care have various problems, which can occur in a number of different combinations. Each of the issues raised, whether individually or in combination with other issues, could equally cause problems for a young person.

GENERAL INFORMATION

SUBSTANCE MISUSE

The term 'substance' refers to legal and illegal drugs and over-the-counter and prescribed medication. 'Drug use', 'misuse' and 'abuse' are often used interchangeably and have a range of meanings including experimental, recreational, socially unacceptable and excessive use of drugs.

'Misuse' is defined by the NHS Health Advisory Service (1996) as "use that is harmful, dependent use or the use of substances as part of a wider spectrum of problematic or harmful behaviour". In these terms, young people who misuse substances may also have significant problems with their psychosocial development.

Possible signs of drug use include changes in:
- appearance
- friends
- interests
- eating
- sleeping habits
- moods.

However, these signs can occur in a young person who is not using drugs, just growing up. Therefore, it is difficult for carers to detect whether a young person is using drugs or not.

Trends in young people's drug use have been reported by the Standing Conference on Drug Abuse (SCODA) & The Children's Legal Centre (1999). Their research indicates that over the past few years, there has been a significant increase in drug use among young people under 18:
- There has been a fivefold increase among 12–13 year olds and an eightfold increase among 14–15 year olds since 1987.
- A small minority of primary school children have tried alcohol, volatile substances and/or an illegal drug.
- One in every two or three young people has tried an illegal drug by the age of 15 (Balding, 1997). This figure rises to almost half of males (48%) and well over a third of females (42%) between the ages of 16 and 19 (Ramsey & Spiller, 1997).

Research indicates that the following trends are being observed in young people's drug use (Balding, 1996, 1997; Ramsey & Spiller, 1997; Social Services Inspectorate, 1997b):
- Most drug use in young people involves cannabis.
- A range of drugs are used by young people, often in combination with alcohol.
- Most drug use is one-off and experimental, but some experimental drug use can be dangerous.
- Regular drug use is less frequent among young people.
- There are regional differences and local variations in patterns and preferences in drug use, which may change rapidly.
- Drug use varies across age groupings and within and between different groups of the same age.
- Young women are using drugs at almost the same rate as young males.
- More young people are starting to experiment with drugs at a younger age.

- In each local authority in England, there is evidence of small but significant numbers of young people with serious drug problems.
- Throughout the country, there are hot spots of young people using heroin and/or injecting drugs.
- The use and methods of use of some drugs is associated with more harm than others, e.g. solvent misuse, combinations of drugs and alcohol, crack use, heroin use and injecting drug use.

According to the NHS Health Advisory Service (1996), some young people are more vulnerable to developing drug problems. A range of factors which could lead to such vulnerability include:

- physiological factors (physical disabilities)
- family factors (family conflict)
- psychological and behavioural factors (early and persistent behavioural problems)
- economic factors (neighbourhood deprivation).

The prevalence of substance misuse problems was generally perceived to be significantly higher among the vulnerable young people in the care of local authorities than among other young people in all the same areas (Social Services Inspectorate, 1997b). According to the report, all local authorities reported small but significant numbers of young people (under 16 years) who were dependent or chaotic drug users in the looked after and supervised population. A particular problem of solvent misuse (in combination with alcohol) was reported among younger teenagers living in children's homes in the majority of areas.

PHYSICAL ABUSE

A large proportion of children who enter the care system have been abused. It is only relatively recently that we have been made aware how frequently this occurs. Children and young people need to be provided with a secure, caring environment. A child who has been physically abused may present with a range of emotional and behavioural problems. These will vary depending on the age of the child or young person. Toddlers tend to show much more angry non-compliance than their peers. They become easily frustrated in tasks or when playing games (Erickson et al, 1989). Older children may become disruptive or aggressive (Shields et al, 1994). Being a victim of any type of abuse or growing up in an atmosphere of violence is thought to distort four areas of a child's functioning: their emotional resilience, attachment, sense of self and peer relationships (Cicchetti & Toth, 1995).

EMOTIONAL ABUSE

Children and young people who have been emotionally abused or deprived may show behavioural changes, especially in a social setting. They can have low self-esteem and feel guilty. They may fail to make friends because they do not have the social skills to do so, or may make friends only with adults. They may have a short attention span and be unable to settle to tasks for more than a few seconds. Children may appear to be hyperactive. In pre-school children, indiscriminate attachment and friendliness is an important indicator of abuse. Abused children may appear to crave physical contact, even with strangers.

In school-age children, severe long-term emotional abuse may affect growth, and they can remain unusually small for their age. When children who are affected in this way are removed from the home, their growth improves, and up to a tenfold increase has been seen in the first few months away from the abusive environment (Skuse, 1989).

(See Section 1 for the issue of sexual abuse.)

TEENAGE PREGNANCIES

The UK has twice as many teenage births as Germany and six times the Dutch rate. In England in 1997, 90,000 teenagers became pregnant – the under-16 year olds accounted for 7,700 births.

In response to the Social Exclusion Unit report (1999), the Government has allocated £60 million to support its recommendations for local and national coordination, improvements in sex education and contraceptive services, and support for pregnant teenagers and teenage parents. The report examined the problem of teenage parenthood and its causes and made some recommendations to develop an integrated strategy to cut rates. The measures proposed may also benefit care leavers, who are also increasingly becoming teenage parents. Some studies have estimated that 25–30% of young women leaving care are mothers.

Social Services are required to demonstrate that they have taken practical steps to prevent teenage pregnancy in their Quality Protects plans. The Department of Health and the Department for Education and Employment are also to produce joint guidance for social workers and youth workers making it clear that they can, and should, direct teenagers to seek advice and contraception if they are sexually active (Daly, 1999).

QUESTIONS, GUIDANCE AND PROFESSIONAL COMMENT

What is the most effective management for crack-cocaine addiction in a young person?

Treatment of cocaine addiction is complex and needs to address a variety of problems. These include polydrug use and drug interactions, infectious disease status, presence of behavioural problems and mental health comorbidity and social, educational and family aspects of the young person's drug misuse. Most often, behavioural and pharmacological approaches are advocated. There are no current medications specifically for crack-cocaine addiction, although several are at an investigative stage. Behavioural interventions comprise mainly providing information, harm reduction and relapse prevention techniques. Contingency management, using voucher-based systems, is showing some promising results. Cognitive–behavioural therapy is another approach used in treatment. However, evidence of effectiveness is derived largely from adult addiction rather than from research specifically on young people. Treatment can be delivered in out-patient or in residential programmes, which are comprehensive and tend to accept those with more severe social, behavioural and mental health problems. An integrated and comprehensive approach that is child protective is the most effective at this time.

Dr Eilish Gilvarry

What can be done to help prevent substance misuse in children and adolescents?

The diversity of drug users and variation in the causes and associated factors require prevention programmes which adopt a variety of approaches. Generally, programmes are broadly focused and aim to promote optimal psychosocial development. Early initiation of educational pro-grammes in primary schools is important. Effective components of these programmes include: intense, long-term involvement with an ability to reinforce gains and to consider booster sessions; a focus on involvement of families, parents and communities; and interactive teaching methods and focus on life skills, problem-solving and decision-making. Targeting programmes at those at greater risk – e.g. those children at risk of school drop-out or mental health problems, or children with parents who use drugs – involves family management, parent training and components that improve educational attendance and self-esteem. Some early promise for these programmes has been shown. Further research is needed to address the role of drugs at different developmental stages in different drug-using careers.

Dr Eilish Gilvarry

Will a young person who has received bad parenting from their own parents need help with their own parenting skills? What are the messages from research?

Parenting, as Smith (1996) points out, "is a complex function involving relationships, communication, social skills, practical skills and the acquisition of understanding". There is now a growing acceptance that all parents can benefit from help with what is a challenging and important role.

Nevertheless, received wisdom and research findings indicate that those who have not been parented well and who do not have suitable role models are likely to need help. The suggestion made more than 25 years ago that "children tend unwittingly to identify with parents and therefore to adopt, when they become parents, the patterns of behaviour towards children that they themselves have experienced during their own childhood" (Bowlby, 1973) has been confirmed by more recent, scientifically-based research (Steele *et al*, 1996). A family history of unemployment, poverty, bad or distressing parental experiences, school failure, parental and family criminal behaviour has been found to be associated with the likelihood of a child following the same route (Farrington & West, 1990; Utting *et al*, 1993). Furthermore, parents who themselves have been in public care are at risk of having their children received into care (Bebbington & Miles, 1989).

It is probable, therefore, that a young person such as Claire will need help to develop their own parenting skills and, moreover, that they will want to improve on their parents' performance. In a recent study comparing a sample of teenagers in public care with a sample living with their families, 53% of those in public care (and 59% of the girls) said they did not intend to look after their children in the same way as their parents had looked after them (Corlyon & McGuire, 1999). This represented a statistically significant difference from the views of their peers not in public care, of whom only 20% (14% of girls) wanted to improve on their parents' child-rearing. Yet the young people in public care were less likely than those in the comparator sample to have learnt about families, relationships, parenting and childcare either in lessons at school or from parents and carers.

However, for young people such as Claire inadequate parenting is not the only issue for consideration. Other negative experiences and events in their lives can adversely affect the way they feel about themselves and their confidence in parenting. In an analysis of data drawn from a longitudinal study, Sweeting & West (1995) found a link between early pregnancy and less time spent with the family; Dryfoos (1990) and Boyer & Fine (1992) suggested that sexual abuse might also increase the likelihood of early pregnancy. Young people who have experienced rejection, disruption or abuse are likely to be emotionally and psychologically vulnerable in ways that may increase the appeal of early parenthood. Yet those who have been abused are least likely to have high levels of self-esteem and confidence, which are vital components of what is commonly termed 'good enough' parenting.

In addition, we must be mindful of the problems typically associated with teenage motherhood. Young single parents tend to come from backgrounds which are characterised by social and economic deprivation, where other alternatives are limited or non-existent and early parenthood provides access to adulthood (Phoenix, 1991; Musick, 1993). Young parents may need greater support with parenting since the 'permitting circumstances' (Rutter, 1974) are likely to be poor. This reflects the fact that the combination of their economic, social and educational circumstances may make parenting more difficult. It does not imply an innate inability to parent because they are young or single: research shows that the quality of relationships and the style and nature of parenting are more important than the type or structure of a family (Pugh *et al*, 1994).

Young mothers who are single parents are more likely to experience lack of support and greater anxiety because of isolation or feelings of dependency (Combes & Schonveld, 1992). While pregnancy and parenthood might bring increased support from previously estranged mothers, it is not always beneficial. It can cause past suspicions and conflicts to rise to the surface and can cause anxieties among professionals about the grandmother's potential to pass on her own inadequate parenting skills to her daughter.

On the other hand, professionals do not always provide sufficient support. Even if there are no obvious child protection issues, social workers tend to switch their interest from the young mother to the baby and to become focused on monitoring child care. Where child protection issues do arise, the primary focus of intervention becomes the child, and a second social worker is not usually allocated to the case, leaving the mother unsupported and her needs unmet (Biehal *et al*, 1993; Corlyon & McGuire, 1999).

Ms Judith Corlyon

Key reading

Substance misuse

American Academy of Child and Adolescents Psychiatry (1997c) Practice parameters for the assessment and treatment of children and adolescents with substance use disorders. *Journal of the American Academy of Child and Adolescents Psychiatry*, **36** (suppl. 10).

Standing Conference on Drug Abuse & The Children's Legal Centre (1999) *Young People and Drugs: Policy Guidance for Drug Interventions*. London: Standing Conference on Drug Abuse.

CHILDREN'S VOICES

Drugs Aint Good Love

It started with a puff
Which wasn't enough
So I had a line
Which made me commit a crime
Then I needed to chill so I took a pill.

I bought a bottle of Bud
Which made me feel rough
So I took some crack
To try and get back.

I didn't know what I was doing
On a spiral down to ruin
I woke up in a hospital bed
With voices swimming around my head.

Scared confused surrounded by tubes
Empty inside with nowhere to hide
Two weeks later I ended up inside
With my freedom denied.

SO REMEMBER DRUGS
AINT GOOD LOVE.

Roxanne, aged 15

'Shout to be Heard'
(Voice for the Child in Care, 1998)

PHYSICAL AND EMOTIONAL ABUSE

Briere, J., Berliner, L., Bulkley, J. A., *et al* (1996) *The American Professional Society on the Abuse of Children (APSAC) Handbook on Child Maltreatment*. Thousand Oaks, CA: Sage.

Glaser, D. (1995) Emotionally abusive experiences. In *Assessment of Parenting: Psychiatric and Psychological Contributions* (eds P. Reder & C. Lucey), pp. 73–86. London: Routledge.

Madge, N. (1997) *Abuse and Survival: A Fact File*. London: The Prince's Trust-Action.

TEENAGE PREGNANCY

Corlyon, J. & McGuire, C. (1999) *Pregnancy and Parenthood: The Views and Experiences of Young People in Public Care*. London: National Children's Bureau.

WHAT'S GOING ON?

GOVERNMENT PROGRAMMES AND GUIDANCE

Quality Protects

This is a major three-year programme which was launched by the Department of Health in November 1998. Quality Protects is about improving the well-being of children in need, which includes those children who are looked after by local authorities (for more information on Quality Protects, see pp. 20–21).

Teenage pregnancy

Objective

> To ensure that children looked after gain maximum life chance benefits from educational opportunities, health care and social care.

One of the sub-objectives is to ensure that children looked after enjoy a standard of health and development as high as that of all children of the same age living in the same area with respect to a number of indicators, one of which is pregnancy in girls aged less than 16 years.

Drug Misuse Special Allocation Fund

(For more information, see p. 21.)

Substance misuse

Target

> To increase the provision of drug treatment services for young people who misuse drugs, particularly the under-18s, and prevention services for vulnerable young people (amongst the under-25s), ensuring that both types of service are provided in the most appropriate ways. This will help to achieve the 10-year drug strategy aim of ensuring that young people from all backgrounds, whatever their culture, gender or race, have access to appropriate programmes; and that the groups of young people most at risk of developing serious drug problems receive appropriate and specific interventions.

CURRENT RESEARCH AND INITIATIVES

CAMHS Mental Illness Specific Grant (MISG)

This grant was first allocated in 1998/1999 to 24 innovative projects (for more information, see p. 21).

Substance misuse

We have identified two local authority projects from the 24 which seem to address this issue.

Lewisham   Aims to provide direct intervention for young offenders and those at risk of offending with mental health needs and substance misuse problems who will not engage with Tier 3 services.

Liverpool   Aims to help young people with serious psychological and emotional needs. The project will focus on 13–16 year olds presenting with a mixture of severe risk including overdose, self-injury, drug misuse and sexual promiscuity. An inter-agency, multi-disciplinary team will provide continuous support 24 hours a day, seven days a week.

Abuse

We have identified two projects from the 24 which seem to address this issue.

Dorset   Aims to provide an effective response to looked after children who have either disclosed abuse, where the young person has experienced significant harm, or where there is a risk of placement breakdown. The project aims to put in place a fast-track mental health service providing a range of interventions including art, drama and music therapies, as well as psychotherapy, counselling and group work.

West Berkshire   Aims to establish a multi-disciplinary team to focus on mental health needs of looked after children and those who are victims of abuse, and provide assessment, consultation and direct therapeutic work.

WHERE TO GO FOR HELP

SUBSTANCE MISUSE

Alcohol

Alcoholics Anonymous
PO Box 1, Stonebow House, Stonebow, York YO1 2NJ.
Tel: 020 7352 3000/1; Tel: 01904 644026.
Website: www.alcoholics-anonymous.org.uk

Alcoholics Anonymous (Ireland)
109 South Circular Road, Leonard's Corner, Dublin, Ireland.
Tel: 00 353(1) 453 8998.

Alcohol Concern
Waterbridge House, 32–36 Loman Street, London SE1 0EE.
Tel: 020 7928 7377; Fax: 020 7928 4644; E-mail: ac@alccon.dircon.co.uk
Website: www.alcoholconcern.org.uk;
Call for your nearest alcohol advisory service.

Al-Anon Family Groups
Tel: 020 7403 0888.
Self-help sessions for people whose lives are affected by someone else's drinking.

Drinkline
Tel: 0345 32 02 02 (Mon-Fri 11am–11pm).
Or dial and listen freecall: 0500 801 802.
Gives confidential information and advice and can put you in touch with local alcohol advice centre.

Drugs

ADFAM National
Waterbridge House, 32–36 Loman Street, London SE1 0EE.
Tel: 020 7928 8898; Fax: 020 7928 8923: Helpline: 020 7928 8900 (Mon–Fri 10am–5pm).
Provides support and information for families and friends of drug users.

Drugs Prevention Advisory Service (DPAS)
DPAS HQ, Room 314, Horseferry House, Dean Ryle Street, London SW1P 2AW.
Tel: 020 7217 8631; Fax: 020 7217 8230.
E-mail: homeofficedpashq@btinternet.com

Families Anonymous
The Doddington & Rollow Community Association, Charlotte Dispard Avenue, london SW11 5JE.
Tel: 020 7498 4680 (Mon–Fri 1pm–5pm); Fax: 020 7498 1990.
Self-help groups around the country for families and friends.

Health Development Agency (formerly the Health Education Authority (HEA))
Trevelyan House, 30 Great Peter Street, London SW1P 2HW.
Tel: 020 7222 5300; Fax: 020 7413 8900.
Website: www.trashed.co.uk/index2.html
This Health Education Authority site, is well presented and provides general information about drugs, relating to any of the following topics: about, origins, effects, the law, composition, emergency and risks.

Drugscope
32–36 Loman Street, London SE1 0EE.

Tel: 020 7928 1211; Fax: 020 7928 1771.
Website: www.drugscope.org.uk;
E-mail: services@drugscope.org.uk
Drugscope has been created through the merger of the UK's foremost drug information and policy organisations: the Institute for the Study of Drug Dependence (ISDD) and the Standing Conference on Drug Abuse (SCODA). Their aim is to infrom drug policy development and reduce drug-related risk. They provide quality drug information, promote effective responses to drug-taking, undertake research at local, national and international levels and advise upon policy-making.

LOCATE, Standing Conference on Drug Abuse
32–36 Loman Street, London SE1 0EE.
Tel: 020 7803 4733.
E-mail: locate@scoda.demon.co.uk
LOCATE (pilot drug education and prevention information service) provides free information for professionals on out-of-school drug education and prevention activities for 11–25 year olds in England.
  LOCATE can help you to:
- obtain information on out-of-school drug education and prevention activities
- contact others who can share their experience
- access sources of funding
- gain support from national organisations
- obtain key guidance on drug education and prevention.

National drugs helpline
Tel: 0800 77 66 00.
Provides information for young people and parents about drugs and solvents. The helpline can also refer young people to their local drugs services. Leaflets that are produced by the HEA and ISDD are available free and include:
- *A Parent's Guide to Drugs and Alcohol: Sources of information and Help*
- *Drugs: The Facts* (for 11–14 year olds)
- *The Score: Facts about Drugs* (for 14–16 year olds)
- *ID-Mag* (for 16–25 year olds)
- *D-Code*– a multimedia CD-ROM with interactive games and information about drugs (for 13–19 year olds). Tel: 01304 614731.

ABUSE

Family Matters
5 Manor Road, Gravesend, Kent DA12 1AA.
Tel: 01474 536661; Helpline: 01474 537392.
Provides counselling and support for survivors of sexual abuse (for adults and children over eight years old).

National Association for People Abused in Childhood (NAPAC)
c/o 42 Curtain Road, London EC2A 3NH.
A postal service for people needing information about help available to survivors of abuse.
National Society for the Prevention of Cruelty to Children
NSPCC Child Protection, 42 Curtain Road, London EC2A 3NH.
Helpline: 0800 800 500 (24 hours); Textphone: 0800 056 0566 (24 hours).
Provides counselling, information and advice to anyone concerned about a child at risk of abuse.

PREGNANCY

Brook Advisory Centres
165 Grays Inn Road, London WC1X 8UD.
Tel: 020 7833 8488; Helpline: 020 7617 8000.

Family Planning Association
2–12 Pentonville Road, London N1 9FP.
Tel: 020 7837 5432; Fax: 020 7837 3042; Helpline: 020 7837 4044.

GENERAL

Careline
Tel: 020 8514 1177 (Mon–Fri 10am–4pm, 7pm–10pm).
Confidential counselling for young people and adults. Can also refer callers to other organisations and support groups throughout the country.

ChildLine
Freepost 1111, London N1 OBR.
Tel: 0800 1111 (24 hours).
Provides confidential counselling, support and advice on any issue.

ChildLine for Children in Care
Freepost 1111, Glasgow G1 1BR.
Tel: 0800 884444.
A special free telephone number for children and young people who are looked after. Provides confidential counselling, support and advice on any issue.

MIND Infoline
Granta House, 15–19 Broadway, Stratford, London E15 4BQ.
Tel: 020 8522 1728 or 08457 660163 (outside London).
Provides information on all aspects of mental health.

The Samaritans
10 The Grove, Slough, Berkshire SL1 1QP.
Tel: 01753 532713; Fax: 01753 775787; Helpline: 0345 909090 (24 hours);
E-mail: jo@samaritans.org
Website: www.samaritans.org.uk
Offers free emotional support to anyone going through difficulties.

Voice for the Child in Care
Unit 4, Pride Court, 80–82 White Lion Street, London N1 9PF.
Tel: 020 7833 5792; Freephone (for young people only): 0808 8005792.
This service offers advocacy (a voice) for children and young people in or leaving care.

Who Cares? LinkLine
Helpline: 0500 56 45 70 (Mon, Wed & Thurs 3.30pm–6.30pm).
Offers information and support to young people who are or who have been in care.

YoungMinds Parents Information Service
2nd Floor, 102–108 Clerkenwell Road, London EC1M 5SA.
Tel: 020 7336 8445; Fax: 020 7336 8446; Helpline: 0345 626376.
This service is for parents or carers with concerns about the mental health or emotional well-being of a child or young person. Provides information and details of local and national services.

Youth Access
2 Taylors Yard, 67 Alderbrook Road, London SW12 8AD.
Tel: 020 8772 9900; fax: 020 8772 9746; E-mail: yaccess@dircon.co.uk
Youth Access can give details and information of counselling services in the child or young person's local area.

"... he has ended up on the streets with no one to turn to."

Dean is 18 years old. He has been in care since the age of 13. Dean and his younger sister went to live with a foster family after their parents died in a fire. Dean never really settled down with the foster family and was returned to a residential home at the age of 15. The foster family, however, adopted his sister.

Just after Dean's 17th birthday, his social worker found him a hostel, and after a few weeks a flat was found for him. However, shortly after he moved into the flat, he lost his job, and with the delays in housing benefit and problems with him signing on, it wasn't long before he was evicted from the flat.

Dean has now ended up homeless with no one to turn to. He has been living on the streets for four months now. His self-esteem is very low and he has begun to drink very heavily.

This vignette raises the issues of bereavement and leaving care. The reader is reminded that many young people in care have various problems, which can occur in a number of different combinations. Each of the issues raised, whether individually or in combination with other issues, could equally cause problems for a young person.

GENERAL INFORMATION

BEREAVEMENT

The loss or death of someone they care for is likely to be deeply distressing for child or young person. 'Bereavement' is the word used to describe the loss that people feel when someone close dies. Grief is the emotion that people go through as a result of the loss of someone they loved.

Each individual's reaction to loss is different and it is impossible to predict how someone will respond. There are certain reactions that are common to both adults and children; these are denial, guilt, anger, fear and physical complaints.

CARE LEAVERS

'Care leavers' are those young people who leave care (cease to be looked after) between the ages of 16 and 18 and who qualify for advice and assistance under Section 24 of the Children Act (Department of Health, 1999).

The average age for leaving home for young people in the population as a whole is 22. Yet every year 4,900 young people leave the care of local authorities when they are aged 16–17, with an increasing number of young people leaving care at 16 (Department of Health, 1999).

Many care leavers receive little support from the local authority, and struggle to cope with independence at such a young age.

- 50–75% of young people leaving care have no educational qualifications (Garrett, 1992) compared with 6% for all school leavers.
- 50% of young people leaving care are unemployed (Broad, 1998).
- 20% experience some form of homelessness within two years of leaving care (Biehal *et al*, 1995).
- 25% of young people in care at one time have some disability (Department of Health, 1999).
- 25–30% of young women leaving care are teenage parents (Department of Health, 1999).

QUESTIONS, GUIDANCE AND PROFESSIONAL COMMENT

What problems may a child or adolescent have following the death of a parent or a close member of the family?

Bereaved children have a range of feelings, such as disbelief, sadness, despair, anger and guilt. Children's responses vary with age:

- Very young children may tantrum more frequently, show anxiety through hyperactivity and show developmental regression.
- Older children are more likely to have nightmares and sleep disturbance. They may show withdrawn or depressed behaviour.

Those aged less than five years also experience feelings of loss, confusion and dislocation. Their lack of understanding and inability to express their feelings makes it harder to reassure them.

Children's grief is not always obvious. It switches on and off quickly – within a short time of expressing sadness, they can cheerfully join in play with friends or participate in other activities. Children may illogically blame themselves for a death in the family. Bereaved children are curious about death. They may ask questions repeatedly as they strive to fully understand.

Adjusting to loss is a long-term process – do not be surprised if children show distress some time later, or want to talk again about the death as they develop emotionally and intellectually and have new experiences. Box 6 lists some important points to remember when caring for a child or young person who is bereaved.

Box 6. Strategies to remember when caring for bereaved children and young people

- Do not insist that children or young people grieve or mourn openly – they may choose not to do so.
- Do not force them to talk when they don't want to.
- Do not avoid their questions as a way of protecting them – find honest, caring and age appropriate explanations.
- Do listen when they want to talk.
- Do check children's beliefs about the death – that way you can reassure them they were not to blame.
- Do give them the information they need, otherwise they will create unhelpful fantasies about what happened.
- Do refer a child for specialist assessment if they have witnessed a traumatic death – they may have symptoms of post-traumatic stress disorder.

Dr Linda Dowdney

What problems do care leavers face and what are the types of service available to these young people?

Most young people, whether they are living with their own families, in foster care or a children's home, experience problems during their journey to adulthood. Care leavers share a lot in common with other young people, but the research evidence points to key differences: they have to leave care and live independently at a much earlier age than other young people leave home; just over a half move regularly and 20% experience homelessness in the two years after they leave care; they have lower levels of educational attainment and lower post-16 further education participation rates; they have higher unemployment rates, more unstable career patterns and higher levels of dependency on welfare benefits; they enter parenthood earlier; and they experience more mental health problems.

With regard to specific groups of care leavers, the largest group of young Black people (i.e. those of Afro-Caribbean, Asian or mixed heritage) leaving care are of mixed heritage. In comparison with young White people, young Black people enter care earlier, stay longer, and after leaving care have similar employment and housing careers. Most young Black people leaving care experience racism.

The evidence from a large number of studies (Stein, 1997) shows that young people leaving care have to cope with the challenges and responsibilities of major changes in their lives – leaving foster and residential care and setting up home, leaving school and entering the world of work or, more likely, being unemployed and surviving on benefits, and being parents – at a far younger age than other young people. They have compressed and accelerated transitions to adulthood.

The increased recognition of the problems faced by care leavers was the consequence of a number of actions by researchers, by the small but powerful voices of young people belonging to 'in care' groups, by campaigners, and by practitioners and managers working with care leavers in the statutory and voluntary agencies. It was this recognition of 'leaving care' issues in the professional and political consciousness that led to the introduction of new leaving care powers and duties through legislative change in England and Wales, Scotland and Northern Ireland during the 1990s.

Social Services provision for care leavers includes specialist leaving care teams, mainstream social work support and projects for specific groups of care leavers. Specialist schemes have developed particularly since the mid-1980s to respond to what have been described as the core needs of care leavers: accommodation, finance, careers and support networks.

Professor Mike Stein

How effective are leaving care services?

This is not an easy question to answer accurately as there are very few studies which have compared the outcomes for care leavers receiving such services with other groups of care leavers. However, the findings of a major English study are broadly consistent with a more substantial study from the USA and point to two ways of answering this question (Biehal *et al*, 1995). Firstly, leaving care schemes can make a positive contribution to specific outcomes for care leavers. They work particularly well in respect of accommodation and life skills including budgeting, negotiating and self-care skills, and to some extent in furthering social networks, developing relationships and building self-esteem. Secondly, researching outcomes has identified other positive influences that are independent of the specialist schemes. Successful educational outcomes are closely linked to placement stability, more often achieved in foster care placements, combined with a supportive and encouraging environment for study. Without such stability and encouragement, post-16 employment and career outcomes are likely to be very poor. Success in social networks, personal relationships and in having a positive self-image, although assisted by schemes, is also closely connected with young people having positive, supportive family relationships with family members or former carers.

Stability, continuity and family and carer links are the foundation upon which specialist leaving care schemes must build if they are to be effective. Schemes also work well by targeting the core needs of care leavers, by being committed to young people and involving them in decision-making, by working with other agencies – particularly housing providers, benefit agencies, and employment and training agencies, influencing policy at the local level – and by operating within a well-developed managerial and policy framework which addresses access to schemes, equal opportunities, service delivery and scheme monitoring. However, research evidence indicates that there is great variation in the resourcing, range and quality of leaving care services within the UK (Broad, 1998).

Finally, there is a failure in much of the leaving care literature to explore theoretical perspectives. Contributions in the area of **attachment theory**, recognising the compensatory stability needs of young people in care, **focal theory**, identifying that the accelerated and compressed transitions of care leavers deny them the psychological opportunities of dealing with major changes over time and a **life course approach**, recognising the interaction between the agency of young people and their wider social contexts, would further enhance our understanding.

Professor Mike Stein

KEY READING

BEREAVEMENT

Dyegrove, A. (1991) *Grief in Children: A Handbook for Adults*. London: Jessica Kingsley.

Smith, S. C. & Pennells, M. (1998) *Interventions with Bereaved Children*. London: Jessica Kingsley.

LEAVING CARE

Biehal, N., Clayden, J., Stein, M., *et al* (1995) *Moving On: Young People and Leaving Care Schemes*. London: HMSO.

Broad, B. (1998) *Young People Leaving Care: Life after the Children Act 1989*. London: Jessica Kingsley.

Stein, M. (1997) *What Works in Leaving Care?* Barkingside: Barnardos.

WHAT'S GOING ON?

GOVERNMENT PROGRAMMES AND GUIDANCE

Quality Protects

This is a major three-year programme which was launched by the Department of Health in November 1998. Quality Protects is about improving the well-being of children in need, which includes those children who are looked after by local authorities (for more information on Quality Protects, see pp. 20–21).

Care leavers

Objective

> To ensure that young people leaving care, as they enter adulthood, are not isolated and participate socially and economically as citizens.

> There are two relevant sub-objectives which local authorities need to consider:
> - for young people who were looked after on their 16th birthday, to maximise the number engaged in education, training or employment at the age of 19; and
> - to maximise the number of young people leaving care after their 16th birthday who are still in touch with SSDs, or a known and approved contact, on their 19th birthday. By 'in touch' is meant a minimum of verbal contact four times during the young person's 19th year. This contact must be recorded.

National Priorities Guidance

This document enhances some of the objectives which have been addressed by Quality Protects by the addition of specific targets (for more information on the National Priorities Guidance, see p. 21).

Care leavers

Target

> To demonstrate that the level of employment, training or education amongst young people aged 19 in 2001/02 who were looked after by Local Authorities in their 17th year on 1 April 1999, is at least 60% of the level amongst that of all young people of the same age in their area.

CURRENT RESEARCH AND INITIATIVES

CAMHS Mental Illness Specific Grant (MISG)

This grant was first allocated in 1998/1999 to 24 innovative projects (for more information, see p. 21).

Care leavers

We have identified one local authority project from the 24 which seems to address the issue of potential mental health problems in care leavers.

Sheffield Aims to help looked after children in residential and foster care, care leavers or those at risk of being in care, with mental health difficulties, by providing therapeutic support.

Other regional studies

Care leavers

Independent Living North East (INLINE)

  A partnership between The Children's Society, Barnardo's and North Tyneside Council, INLINE North Tyneside is a project designed to help homeless or potentially homeless young people and care leavers make the transition to independent living.

Touchstone House
2–4 Middleton Crescent, Leeds LS11 6JU.
Tel: 0113 271 8277; Fax: 0113 270 0072.

  A community mental health service and housing provider which has developed specific initiatives to benefit young people.

WHERE TO GO FOR HELP

BEREAVEMENT

Compassionate Friends
53 North Street, Bristol BS3 1EN.
Tel: 0117 966 5202; Fax: 0117 914 4368: Helpline: 0117 953 9639: E-mail: info@tcf.org.uk; Website: www.tcf.org.uk

Cruse Bereavement Care
126 Sheen Road, Richmond, Surrey TW9 1UR.
Helpline: 020 8332 7227 (Mon–Fri 9.30am–5pm)

HOMELESSNESS

Centrepoint Central Office
Bewlay House, 2 Swallow Place, London W1R 7AA.
Tel: 020 7629 2426 5300.
Website: www.centrepoint.org.uk
'Centrepoint' is a registered charity and housing association which aims to ensure that no young people are at risk because they do not have a safe place to stay.
(Tel: 020 7544 5000 for a free publication, *Leaving Home Guide*. This contains useful

information for young people when they are first living independently.)
First Key (The National Leaving Care Advisory Service)
Oxford Chambers, Oxford Place, Leeds LS1 3AX.
Tel: 0113 244 3898; Fax: 0113 243 2541.
First Key exists to significantly improve the life chances of young people in and leaving care, through influencing and providing quality services to those with particular responsibility for this potentially vulnerable group. Helps young people leaving the public system to live independently.

The London Connection
12 Adelaide Street, London WC2N 4HW.
Tel: 020 7321 0633; Fax: 020 7839 6277.
A large resource centre providing a wide range of services to homeless 16–25 year olds, with input from two full-time mental health workers.

Shelter
The National Campaign for Homeless People, 88 Old Street, London EC1V 9HU.
Tel: 020 7505 4699; Shelterline: 0800 446441 (24 hours a day, seven days a week).
Website: www.shelter.org.uk

GENERAL

Careline
Tel: 020 8514 1177 (Mon–Fri 10am–4pm, 7pm–10pm).
Confidential counselling for young people and adults. Can also refer callers to other organisations and support groups throughout the country.

MIND Infoline
Granta House, 15–19 Broadway, Stratford, London E15 4BQ.
Tel: 020 8522 1728 or 08457 660163 (outside London).
Provides information on all aspects of mental health.

The Samaritans
10 The Grove, Slough, Berkshire SL1 1QP.
Tel: 01753 532713; Fax: 01753 775787; Helpline: 0345 909090 (24 hours);
E-mail: jo@samaritans.org; Website: www.samaritans.org.uk
Offers free emotional support to anyone going through difficulties.

Voice for the Child in Care
Unit 4, Pride Court, 80–82 White Lion Street, London N1 9PF.
Tel: 020 7833 5792; Freephone (for young people only): 0808 8005792.
This service offers advocacy (a voice) for children and young people in or leaving care.

Who Cares? LinkLine
Tel: 020 7251 3117; Helpline: 0500 56 45 70 (Mon, Wed & Thurs 3.30pm–6.30pm).
Offers information and support to young people who are or who have been in care.

Youth Access
2 Taylors Yard, 67 Alderbrook Road, London SW12 8AD.
Tel: 020 8772 9900; Fax: 020 8772 9746; E-mail: yaccess@dircon.co.uk
Youth Access can give details and information of counselling services in the child or young person's local area.

Glossary

Anhedonia The inability to feel pleasure or happiness in response to experiences that are ordinarily pleasurable. Often a characteristic of major depression.

Antidepressant drugs Drugs used to alleviate the symptoms of depression. Examples include tricyclics such as imipramine (Tofranil), monoamine oxidase inhibitors (MAOIs) such as phenelzine (Nardil), and selective serotonin reuptake inhibitors (SSRIs) such as fluoxetine (Prozac).

Antipsychotic drugs Drugs used to alleviate the symptoms of conditions such as schizophrenia. Examples include typical antipsychotics such as chlorpromazine (Thorazine), and atypical antipsychotics such as risperidone (Resperdal). The newer atypical antipsychotics are thought to have superior effects to other classes of antipsychotic drugs and also to have fewer side-effects.

Behavioural therapy This therapy uses psychological principles to achieve behavioural goals. It is often contrasted with *psychodynamic psychotherapy*, where the focus is more on achieving insight or personality change.

Cognition The mental process characterised by knowing, thinking, learning, understanding and judging.

Cognitive therapy Any of the methods of treating disorders that help a person to change attitudes, perceptions and patterns of thinking from rational to realistic thoughts about self and situations.

Cognitive–behavioural therapy (CBT) Describes the combination of behaviour therapy and cognitive therapy in which, usually, behavioural procedures are used to change cognitive processes.

Looked after Children Act term for children for whom the local authority is providing accommodation or care.

Psychoanalysis A method of psychological treatment, developed from the work of Freud, which focuses on uncovering the unconscious conflicts by mainly verbal means. It is classically a lengthy and intensive therapy lasting several years, although briefer and less intensive forms have also been developed.

Psychoanalytic 1. relating to psychoanalysis; 2. using the techniques or principles of psychoanalysis in an attempt to examine causality.

Psychodynamic   A term derived from psychoanalytic theory which describes the interplay of mental and emotional forces and the way these affect behaviour and mental state.

Psychodynamic therapy   This form of therapy has its recent origins in Freud's work. It attempts to "approach the patient empathetically from the inside in order to help him identify and understand what is happening in his inner world in relation to his background, upbringing and development".

Psychoeducation   Aims to provide information and increase a patient's understanding of a problem. The sharing of information within a therapeutic relationship has two functions: the knowledge gained assists in orienting the patient towards reality; and the awareness of newly learned facts may have a direct impact on the patient's emotional state and consequently their behaviour.

Psychopathology   1. the behavioural manifestations of any mental disorder; 2. the study of the causes, processes and manifestations of any mental disorder.

Psychosocial   Pertaining to a combination of psychological and social factors.

Psychosocial development   A description of the normal serial development or trust, autonomy, initiative, industry, identity, intimacy, generativity and integrity. For the child to reach a new stage successfully, the tasks of the proceeding one should be fully mastered.

Psychotherapy   Any of a large number of related methods of treating mental and emotional disorders by psychological techniques rather than physical approaches.

References

American Academy of Child and Adolescent Psychiatry (1994) Practice parameters for the assessment of children and adolescents with schizophrenia. *Journal of the American Academy of Child and Adolescent Psychiatry*, **33**, 616–635.

—— (1997*a*) Practice parameters for the assessment and treatment of children and adolescents with conduct disorder. *Journal of the American Academy of Child and Adolescent Psychiatry*, **36** (suppl. 10).

—— (1997*b*) Practice parameters for the assessment and treatment of children and adolescents with bipolar disorder. *Journal of the American Academy of Child and Adolescent Psychiatry*, **36** (suppl. 10).

—— (1997*c*) Practice parameters for the assessment and treatment of children and adolescents with substance use disorders. *Journal of the American Academy of Child and Adolescent Psychiatry*, **36** (suppl. 10).

—— (1998) Practice parameters for the assessment and treatment of children and adolescents with depressive disorders. *Journal of the American Academy of Child and Adolescent Psychiatry*, **37** (suppl. 10).

Ainsworth, M. D. S., Blehar, M., Waters, E., *et al* (1978) *Patterns of Attachment: A Psychological Study of the Strange Situation*. Hillsdale, NJ: Lawrence Erlbaum.

Audit Commission (1996) *Misspent Youth: Young People and Crime*. London: Audit Commission.

—— (1999) *Children in Mind: Child and Adolescent Mental Health Services*. London: Audit Commission.

Ayotte, W. (1998) *Supporting Unaccompanied Children in the Asylum Process*. London: Save the Children.

Balding, J. (1996) *Young People and Illegal Drugs in 1989–1995: Facts and Predictions*. Exeter: Schools Health Education Unit.

—— (1997) *Young People and Illegal Drugs in 1996*. Exeter: Schools Health Education Unit.

Banks, N. J. (1996) Young single white mothers with black children in therapy. *Clinical Child Psychology and Psychiatry*, **1**, 19–28.

Barlow, J. (1997) *Systematic Review of the Effectiveness of Parent Training Programmes in Improving Behavioural Problems in Children Aged 3–10 Years*. Oxford: Department of Public Health, Health Services Research Unit.

Barn, R., Sinclair, R. & Ferdinand, D. (1997) *Acting on Principle: An Examination of Race and Ethnicity in Social Services Provision for Children and Families*. London: British Agencies for Adoption and Fostering.

Bebbington, J. & Miles, A. (1989) Children who enter local authority care. *British Journal of Social Work*, **19**, 349–368.

Belsky, J. & Cassidy, J. (1994) Attachment: theory and practice. In *Development Through Life: A Handbook for Clinicians* (eds M. Rutter & D. Hay), pp. 373–402. Oxford: Blackwell Science.

Berliner, L. & Saunders, B. (1996) Treating fear and anxiety in sexually abused children: results of a controlled, two year follow-up study. *Child Maltreatment*, **1**, 294–309.

Berridge, D. & Brodie, I. (1997) An exclusive education. *Community Care* (suppl.), **1156**, 4–5.

Biehal, N., Clayden, J., Stein, M., *et al* (1995) *Moving On: Young People and Leaving Care Schemes*. London: The Sationery Office.

Black, D., Harris-Hendricks, J. & Wolkind, S. (1998) *Child Psychiatry and the Law*. London: Gaskell.

Bowlby, J. (1969/1982) *Attachment and Loss: Attachment*. New York: Basic Books.

—— (1973) *Separation: Anxiety and Anger*. London: Hogarth Press.

—— (1988) *A Secure Base: Clinical Implications of Attachment Theory*. London: Routledge & Kegan Paul.

Boyer, D. & Fine, M. (1992) Sexual abuse as a factor in adolescent pregnancy and child maltreatment. *Family Planning Perspectives*, **24**, 4–11.

Briere, J., Berliner, L., Bulkley, J. A., *et al* (1996) *The ASPAC Handbook on Child Maltreatment*. Thousand Oaks, CA: Sage.

Broad, B. (1998) *Young People Leaving Care: Life after the Children Act 1989*. London: Jessica Kingsley.

Butler, J. & Vostanis, P. (1998) Characteristics of referrals to a mental health service for young people in care. *Psychiatric Bulletin*, **22**, 85–87.

Cicchetti, D. & Toth, S. L. (1995) A developmental psychopathological perspective on child abuse and neglect. *Journal of the American Academy of Child and Adolescent Psychiatry*, **35**, 1402–1410.

Cliffe, D. & Berridge, D. (1991) *Closing Children's Homes*. London: National Children's Bureau.

Cohen, J. A. & Mannarino, A. P. (1997) A treatment outcome study for sexually abused preschool children during a one-year follow-up. *Journal of the American Academy of Child and Adolescent Psychiatry*, **36**, 1228–1235.

Combes, G. & Schonveld, A. (1992) *Life Will Never Be the Same Again*. London: Health Education Authority.

Cooper, A. & Webb, L. (1999) Out of the maze: permanency planning in a post-modern world. *Journal of Social Work Practice*, **13**, 120–134.

Corbett, J. A. (1979) Psychiatric morbidity and mental retardation. In *Psychiatric Illness and Mental Handicap* (eds F. E. James & R. P. Snaith). London: Gaskell.

Corlyon, J. & McGuire, C. (1999) *Pregnancy and Parenthood: the Views and Experiences of Young People in Public Care*. London: National Children's Bureau.

Daly, N. (1999) Councils that fail to prevent teenage pregnancies may lose out on money. *Community Care*, **1277**, 4–5.

Davies, C. (1998) Developing interests in child care outcome measurement: a central Government perspective. *Children and Society*, **12**, 155–160.

Deblinger, E., McLeer, S. V., Atkins, M. S., *et al* (1989) Post-traumatic stress in sexually abused, physically abused, and non-abused children. *Child Abuse and Neglect*, **13**, 403–408.

——, Lippman, J. & Steer, R. (1996) Sexually abused children suffering post-traumatic stress symptoms: initial treatment outcome findings. *Child Maltreatment*, **1**, 310–321.

Department for Education and Employment (1999) *The Education of Children Being Looked After by Local Authorities*. London: Department for Education and Employment.

Department of Health (1995) Looking After Children: Assessment and Action Records. London: HMSO.

—— (1998*a*) *Caring for Children Away from Home: Messages from Research*. Chichester: John Wiley.

—— (1998*b*) *The Quality Protects Programme: Transforming Children's Services. Local Authority Circular LAC(98)22*. London: Department of Health.

—— (1998*c*) *Modernising Health and Social Services: National Priorities Guidance 1999/00–2001/02. Health Service Circular HSC(98)159; Local Authority Circular LAC(98)22*. London: Department of Health.

—— (1999a) *Framework for the Assessment of Children in Need and their Families*. London: HMSO.

—— (1999b) *Me, Survive, Out There? New Arrangements for Young People Living in and Leaving Care*. London: Department of Health.

—— (1999c) *Drug Misuse Special Allocation: 1999/2000: Funding and Guidance on the Modernisation Fund Element. Health Service Circular HSC 1999/036*. London: Department of Health.

—— (1999d) *NHS Modernisation Fund and Mental Health Grant for Child and Adolescent Mental Health Services 1999/2002. Health Service Circular HSC 1999/126; Local Authority Circular LAC(99)22*. London: Department of Health.

Dryfoos, J. (1990) *Adolescents at Risk: Prevalence and Prevention*. Oxford: Oxford University Press.

Dyegrove, A. (1991) *Grief in Children: A handbook for Adults*. London: Jessica Kingsley.

Education Act (1993) London: HMSO.

Erickson, M., Egeland, B. & Pianta, R. (1989) The effects of maltreatment on the development of young children. In *Child Maltreatment: Theory and Research on the Causes and Consequences of Child Abuse and Neglect* (eds D. Cicchetti & V. Carlson). New York: Cambridge University Press.

Fahlberg, V. (1994) *A Child's Journey Through Placement*. London: British Association of Adoption and Fostering.

Falkov, A. (ed.) (1998) *Crossing Bridges: Training Resources for Working with Mentally Ill Parents and their Children. Reader for Managers, Practitioners and Trainers*. London: Department of Health.

Farmer, E. & Pollock, S. (1998) *Sexually Abused and Abusing Children in Substitute Care*. Chichester: Wiley.

Farrington, D. & West, D. (1990) *The Cambridge Study in Delinquent Development: A Long-Term Follow-Up of 411 London Males in Criminality, Personality, Behaviour and Life History*. Berlin: Springer-Verlag.

Feldman, R. A., Caplinger, T. E. & Wodarski, J. S. (1983) *The St. Louis Conundrum: The Effective Treatment of Antisocial Youths*. Englewood Cliffs, NJ: Prentice Hall.

Fergusson, D. M. & Mullen, P. E. (1999) *Childhood Sexual Abuse: An Evidence Based Perspective*. Thousand Oaks, CA: Sage.

Fonagy, P., Steele, M., Steele, H., *et al* (1994) The theory and practice of resilience. *Journal of Child Psychology and Psychiatry*, **35**, 231–257.

Garrett, L. (1992) *Leaving Care and After*. London: National Children's Bureau.

Gillberg, C., Persson, E., Grufman, E., *et al* (1986) Psychiatric disorders in mildly and severly mentally retarded urban children and adolescents: epidemiological aspects. *British Journal of Psychiatry*, **149**, 68–74.

Goh, S. & Holland, A. J. (1994) A framework for commissioning services for people with learning disabilities. *Journal of Public Health Medicine*, **16**, 279-285.

Goodyer, I. (ed.) (1995) *The Depressed Child and Adolescent: Developmental and Clinical Perspectives*. Cambridge: Cambridge University Press.

Glaser, D. (1995) Emotionally abusive experiences. In *Assessment of Parenting: Psychiatric and Psychological Contributions* (eds P. Reder & C. Lucey), pp. 73–86. London: Routledge.

Graham, P. (1991) *Child Psychiatry: A Developmental Approach*. Oxford: Oxford University Press.

—— & Hughes, C. (1997) *So Young, So Sad, So Listen*. London: Gaskell/West London Health Promotion Agency.

Grinberg, L. & Grinberg, R. (1989) *Psychoanalytic Perspective on Migration and Exile*. London: Yale University Press.

Gunn, J., Maden, A. & Swinton, M. (1991) Treatment needs of prisoners with psychiatric disorders. *British Medical Journal*, **303**, 338–341.

Hagell, A. & Newburn, T. (1994) *Persistent Young Offenders*. London: Policy Studies Institute.

Harrington, R., Fudge, H., Rutter, M., *et al* (1990) Adult outcomes of childhood and adolescent depression: I. Psychiatric status. *Archives of General Psychiatry*, **47**, 465–473.

——, Whittaker, J., Shoebridge, P., *et al* (1998) Systematic review of efficacy of cognitive behaviour therapies in child and adolescent depressive disorder. *British Medical Journal*, **316**, 1559–1563.

——, Whittaker, J. & Shoebridge, P. (1998) Psychological treatment of depression in children and adolescents: a review of treatment research. *British Journal of Psychiatry*, **173**, 291–298.

Hazell, P., O'Connell, D., Heathcote, D., *et al* (1995) Efficacy of tricyclic drugs in treating child and adolescent depression: a meta-analysis. *British Medical Journal*, **310**, 897–901.

Hodges, J. & Tizard, B. (1989*a*) Social and family relationships of ex-institutional adolescents. *Journal of Child Psychology and Psychiatry*, **30**, 77–97.

—— & —— (1989*b*) IQ and behavioural adjustment of ex-institutional adolescents. *Journal of Child Psychology and Psychiatry*, **30**, 53–75.

House of Commons Health Committee (1998) *Children Looked After by Local Authorities: Health Committee Second Report: Volume 1: Session 1997–98*. London: House of Commons.

Howe, D. (1995) *Attachment Theory for Social Work Practice*. Basingstoke: Macmillan.

——, Brandon, M., Hinings, D., *et al* (1999) *Attachment Theory, Child Maltreatment and Family Support: A Practice and Assessment Model*. Basingstoke: Macmillan.

Hunter, M. (1993) The emotional needs of children in care – an overview. *Association of Child Psychology and Psychiatry*, **15**, 214–218.

Jones, D. P. H. & Ramchandani, P. (1999) *Child Sexual Abuse: Informing Practice from Research*. Oxford: Radcliffe Medical Press.

Joughin, C., Jarrett, L. & MacLean Steel, K. (1999) *Who's Who in Child and Adolescent Mental Health Services*. London: Focus.

Kazdin, A. E. (1995) *Conduct Disorders in Childhood and Adolescence*. London: Sage.

Kendall-Tackett, K. A., Williams, L. M. & Finkelhor, D. (1993) Impact of sexual abuse on children: a review and synthesis of recent empirical studies. *Psychological Bulletin*, **113**, 164–180.

Kurtz, Z., Thornes, R. & Wolkind, S. (1996) *Services for the Mental Health of Children and Young People in England: Assessment of Needs and Unmet Need*. London: South West Thames Region Health Authority.

Local Government Drugs Forum & Standing Conference On Drug Abuse (1997) *Drug Using Parents Policy and Guidelines for Inter-agency Working*. London: Local Government Association Publications.

Lochman, J. E., Lampron, L. B., Gemmer, T. C., *et al* (1989) Teacher consultation and cognitive–behavioural interventions with aggressive boys. *Psychology in the Schools*, **26**, 179–188.

Madge, N. (1997) *Abuse and Survival: A Fact File*. London: The Prince's Trust Action.

McCann, J. B., James, A., Wilson, S., *et al* (1996) Prevalence of psychiatric disorders in young people in the care system. *British Medical Journal*, **313**, 1529–1530.

Mental Health Foundation (1999) *Bright Futures: Promoting Children and Young People's Mental Health*. London: Mental Health Foundation.

Merry, S. N. & Andrews, L. K. (1994) Psychiatric status of sexually abused children twelve months after disclosure of abuse. *Journal of the American Academy of Child and Adolescent Psychiatry*, **33**, 939–944.

Monck, E., Bentovim, A. & Goodall, G. (1993) *Child Sexual Abuse: A Descriptive and Treatment Study*. London: HMSO.

Morgan, S. (1999) *Care about Education: A Joint Training Curriculum for Supporting Children in Public Care*. London: National Children's Bureau.

Mounteney, J. (1998) *Children of Drug-Using Parents. Highlight no. 163*. London: National Children's Bureau.

Musick, J. (1993) *Young, Poor and Pregnant: The Psychology of Teenage Motherhood*. New Haven, MA: Yale University Press.

NHS Centre for Reviews and Dissemination, University of York (1998) Deliberate self-harm. *Effective Health Care*, **4**, 1–12.

National Health Service Health Advisory Service (1994) *Suicide Prevention: A Manual of Guidance for the Purchasers and Providers of Mental Health Care*. London: HMSO.

—— (1995) *Together We Stand: Thematic Review on the Commissioning, Role and Management of Child and Adolescent Mental Health Services*. London: HMSO.

—— (1996) *Children and Young People: Substance Misuse Services: The Substance of Young Need*. London: The Stationery Office.

Offord, D. R. & Bennett, K. J. (1994) Conduct disorder: long-term outcomes and intervention effectiveness. *Journal of the American Academy of Child and Adolescent Psychiatry*, **33**, 1069–1078.

O'Hanlon, L. & Ejioforj, J. (1999) Should we encourage transracial adoption? *The Guardian*, 23/10/99.

Owens, D. & House, A. (1994) General hospital services for deliberate self-harm. *Journal of the Royal College of Physicians*, **28**, 370–371.

Owusu-Bempah, J. (1994) Race, self-identity and social work. *British Journal of Social Work*, **24**, 123–136.

Pearce, J. & Holmes, S. P. (1994) *Health Gain Investment Programme. Technical Review Document. People with Mental Health Problems (Part Four) – Child and Adolescent Mental Health*. London: NHS Executive Trent and Centre for Mental Health Services Development.

Philips, J. (1997) Meeting the psychiatric needs of children in foster care: social workers' views. *Psychiatric Bulletin*, **21**, 609–611.

Phoenix, A. (1991) *Young Mothers?* Cambridge: Polity Press.

Pugh, G. De'Arth, E. & Smith, C. (1994) *Confident Parents, Confident Children*. London: National Children's Bureau.

Quinn, P. (1997) *Understanding Disability: A Lifespan Approach*. Thousand Oaks, CA: Sage.

Ramsey, M. & Spiller, J. (1997) *Drug Misuse Declared in 1996: Latest results from the British Crime Survey, Research Study 172*. London: HMSO.

Royal College of Psychiatrists (1998a) *Managing Deliberate Self-Harm in Young People (CR64)*. London: Royal College of Psychiatrists.

—— (1998b) *Psychiatric Services for Children and Adolescents with a Learning Disability (CR70)*. London: Royal College of Psychiatrists.

Rutter, M. (1974) *Dimensions of parenthood: some myths and some suggestions*. In *The Family in Society*. London: HMSO.

—— & Quinton, D. (1984) Parental psychiatric disorder: effects on children. *Psychological Medicine*, **14**, 853–880.

——, Giller, H. & Haggell, A. (1998) *Antisocial Behaviour by Young People*. Cambridge: Cambridge University Press.

——, Tizard, J., Yule. W., *et al* (1976) Isle of Wight Studies 1964–1974. *Psychological Medicine*, **7**, 313–332.

Scott, S. (1998) Aggressive behaviour in childhood. *British Medical Journal*, **316**, 202–206.

Shaw, C. (1998) *Remember My Messages*. London: The Who Cares? Trust.

Shields, A. M., Ryan, R. M. & Cicchetti, D. (1994) The development of emotional and behavioural self regulation and social competence among maltreated school children. *Developmental Psychopathology*, **6**, 57–75.

Skuse, D. (1989) Psychosocial adversity and impaired growth: in search of causal mechanisms. In *The Scope of Epidemiological Psychiatry: Essays in Honour of Michael Shepherd*, pp. 240–263. London: Routledge.

Smith, C. (1996) *Developing Parenting Programmes*. London: National Children's Bureau.

Smith, S. C. & Pennells, M. (1998) *Interventions with Bereaved Children*. London: Jessica Kingsley.

Social Exclusion Unit (1998) *Truancy and School Exclusion*. London: HMSO.

—— (1999) *Teenage Pregnancy*. London: HMSO.

Social Services Inspectorate (1997a) *When Leaving Home is Also Leaving Care: An Inspection of Services for Young People Leaving Care. CI(97)4*. London: Department of Health.

—— (1997b) *Young People and Substance Misuse: The Local Authority Response*. London: Department of Health.

Spacarelli, S. & Kim, S. (1995) Resilience criteria and factors associated with resilience in sexually abused girls. *Child Abuse and Neglect*, **19**, 1171–1182.

Standing Conference On Drug Abuse & The Children's Legal Centre (1999) *Young People and Drugs: Policy Guidance for Drug Interventions*. London: Standing Conference On Drug Abuse.

Steele, H., Steele, M. & Fonagy, P. (1996) Associations among attachment classifications of infants, mothers and fathers. *Child Development*, **67**, 542–555.

Stein, M. (1997) *What Works in Leaving Care?* Barkingside: Barnardos.

Sweeting, H. & West, P. (1995) Family life and health in adolescence: a role for culture in the health inequalities debate? *Social Science and Medicine*, **40**, 163–175.

Tebbutt, J., Swanston, H., Oates, R. K., *et al* (1997) Five years after child sexual abuse: persisting dysfunction and problems of prediction. *Journal of the American Academy of Child and Adolescent Psychiatry*, **36**, 330–339.

Troy, M. & Sroufe, L. A. (1987) Victimization among preschoolers: role of attachment relationship history. *Journal of the American Academy of Child and Adolescent Psychiatry*, **26**, 166–172.

United Nations High Commissioner for Refugees (1994) *Refugee Children: Guidelines on Protection and Care*. Geneva: United Nations High Commissioner for Refugees.

Utting, D., Bright, J. & Henricson, C. (1993) *Crime and the Family: Improving Child-Rearing and Preventing Delinquency*. London: Family Policy Studies Centre.

Voice for the Child in Care (1998) *Sometimes You've Got to Shout to be Heard*. London: Voice for the Child in Care.

Wallace, S. A., Crown, J. M., Cox, A. D., *et al* (1997) *Child and Adolescent Mental Health: Health Care Needs Assessment*. Oxford: Radcliffe Medical Press.

Webster-Stratton, C. (1993) Strategies for helping early school-aged children with oppositional defiant and conduct disorders: the importance of home–school partnerships. *School Psychology Review*, **22**, 437–457.

—— & Hammond, M. (1997) Treating children with early-onset conduct problems: a comparison of child and parent training interventions. *Journal of Consulting and Clinical Psychology*, **65**, 93–109.

White, J., Moffit, T., Earls, F., *et al* (1990) Preschool predictors of persistent conduct disorder and delinquency. *Criminology*, **28**, 443–454.

The Who Cares? Trust & Calouste Gulbenkian Foundation (1999) *Equal Chances: Project Summary*. London: Who Cares? Trust.

World Health Organization (1992) *The ICD–10 Classification of Mental and Behavioural Disorders: Clinical Descriptions and Diagnostic Guidelines. (ICD–10)*. Geneva: WHO.

Appendices

Summaries of regional projects and initiatives examining the health and mental health of looked after children

IDENTIFYING THE ROLE OF COMMUNITY PAEDIATRICS AND SCHOOL NURSING IN MEETING THE HEALTH AND MENTAL HEALTH NEEDS OF YOUNG PEOPLE IN RESIDENTIAL CARE IN CHESHIRE

The study had two aims:
- to identify whether there are gaps in knowledge about the health-related needs of one group of teenagers in a residential children's home which could be filled by a community paediatric service; and
- to identify what these young people see as important in terms of health information.

Data were collected for a three-month period on the residents of a children's home, using information from the home records and comparing it with information from the child health records. A health information topics list was completed by the young people and semi-structured interviews with individual residents were recorded on audiotape.

Data from the children's home records were collected for 36 residents and child health records were obtained for 29.

The health information topics list was completed by 22 residents and 18 were interviewed. Child health records provided the only information on 53% of child protection registrations and 17.5% of statements of special educational needs. Most information on birth history, developmental and early medical history, immunisations, growth, hearing and colour vision came from child health records. The following were present in residents:
- emotional and behavioural problems in 100%;
- criminal activity in 75%;
- substance misuse in 45%;
- smoking in 47%; and
- alcohol misuse in 50%.

This information was known to the home, as was the information about 17 of the 20 with current medical problems. Poor use of looked after children records was identified, together with a paucity of information in both home records and child health records about results of annual medicals of looked after children. The young people wanted information on mental health issues, keeping fit, substance use and sexual health. Written information was preferred by 72%. Puberty, acne and eating disorders were also of concern. Telephone helpline numbers need to be Freephone numbers. Reluctance to request appointments for personal matters was identified, together with lack of encouragement or opportunity to ask about personal health concerns during medical examinations.

In conclusion, important information about the health needs of looked after young people was not known to the home. Community paediatricians should be proactive in identifying and addressing these needs. A school nurse health interview could identify individual information needs and facilitate access to other health professionals. A school nurse 'drop-in' clinic should be developed and a health information pack produced for every resident. A designated doctor for looked after children could facilitate exchange of information about specific children, and have an advocacy role for these children. Improved exchange of information is needed between Social Services, Health and Education. Use of looked after children records should be improved and use of information obtained from annual medicals of looked after children audited.

Dr Annabelle Bundle, Associate Specialist-Community Paediatrics

For a copy of the paper and further information, contact Dr Annabelle Bundle, Cheshire Community Healthcare Trust, Barony Road, Nantwich, Cheshire CW5 5QU.

HEALTH CARE OF LOOKED AFTER CHILDREN INITIATIVE IN LINCOLNSHIRE

There are two child and adolescent mental health teams in Lincolnshire and both of them are taking part in a scheme funded jointly by Health and Social Services to better meet the health needs of young people accommodated in children's homes.

The initiative came about after a joint Lincolnshire County Council (LCC) and Health working party reviewed the needs of children and young people looked after by LCC in 1996. The working party proposed a jointly funded initiative to better meet the needs of these children and young people. In keeping with a pre-existing multi-agency strategy for children suffering from mental health problems, the two health trusts providing child and adolescent mental health services (CAMHS) in the county developed several jointly funded nurse specialist posts. The post-holders' role was to provide advice and guidance on the management of children and young people in children's homes who have mental health problems, to offer case discussions with care staff and to liaise with other health professionals who are involved with particular children.

This initiative is now an intrinsic part of the looked after team of health, social services and educational professionals. The two CAMHS services have developed the scheme somewhat differently. In the North, all of our nurse specialists share the looked after children role, and each children's home has a named nurse who visits weekly. Consultant child psychiatrists provide consultation to the nursing staff as required. Children and young people with significant mental health problems are discussed during the nurses' weekly visits. If referral to the CAMHS team seems appropriate, then the child or young person is referred and seen in the usual way.

The CAMHS work in the North has been paralleled by the development of the role of child health doctors, who have taken on duties of providing health surveillance, statutory medical examinations and medical advice to a designated children's home. An improved system of medical record-keeping has been developed in order to enable children and young people to have a personal understanding of health care issues. This part of the initiative has been offered on a revenue-neutral basis as part of a reorganisation of community paediatrics within the Trust.

The health care of looked after children initiative began operating in March 1998 and a joint agency review was planned for October 1999. Overall, practitioners in both health and social services feel positive about this work. There has been better liaison and more appropriate contacts with children's own GPs. Referrals of children and young people who are living in children's homes to the CAMHS team are now almost appropriate, and team members usually know quite a lot about these young people by the time they are seen for assessment. Crisis calls from children's homes have been reduced.

Anne Thompson, Consultant Child and Adolescent Psychiatrist,
Lincoln District Healthcare NHS Trust

Maureen Laing, Clinical Nurse Specialist, Lincoln District Healthcare NHS Trust

Colin Pitman, Service Manager-Residential Care,
Lincolnshire County Council Social Services Directorate

SUMMARY OF THE *REPORT OF THE PROGRAMME TEAM FOR HEALTH NEEDS OF YOUNG PEOPLE IN RESIDENTIAL CARE 1992–1997 IN NOTTINGHAM*

The programme began in 1992 as a joint venture between Health and Social Services in Nottingham to develop a high-quality coordinated service that will assess in partnership with the young people their health needs and ensure that they are met.

A pilot study was carried out in one community home in 1992. A core team was established in 1994 and commenced work in 1995. This consisted of three new appointments of a research school nurse (full-time), clinical psychologist and administrator (both part-time) and input from a community paediatrician, a child and adolescent psychiatrist, a Social Services policy officer and an educational psychologist employed by Social Services.

The programme was established in recognition of the unmet needs of these children. Three areas of work were addressed:

1   To gain a more comprehensive assessment of the physical and mental health needs of young people in community homes, a series of standardised questionnaires was given to each young person and/or their keyworker. Initially, the questionnaires were given out to the young people in paper form. However, owing to many young people refusing to complete the questionnaires or returning them partially completed, the questionnaires were subsequently transferred to a laptop computer that was taken into the homes. The young people were much more willing to complete the questionnaires in this form.

   The findings of these questionnaires are fed back to the young people, and recommendations are developed jointly for an individual health care plan. Implementation is monitored through monthly core group meetings.

   Thirty-nine mental health assessments across seven children's homes had been completed on the computer when the report had been published. Participants ranged from 9–16 years old (mean age 14) and included 28 males and 11 females. Preliminary results indicated a high level of fear and anxiety in the young people looked after (over 75% with significant levels of anxiety) and high levels of depression (nearly 44% of the young people showing clinical significant levels). Also, 46% of the young people interviewed demonstrated significant low levels of perceived control.

2 Training programmes have been developed for residential social workers. The course runs over six days covering important physical, mental and community health topics. To date, over half the residential social workers in Nottingham have received this training. Follow-up confirms the educational value of these courses.

3 This group of very needy young people misses out on school health services, including health promotion and immunisation, often as a result of poor school attendance and frequent moves. Health promotion provides a vital part of each young person's care plan as it addresses important issues linked to life skills. Part of the role of the research school nurses linked to the community home, within the project, was to offer a health promotion package acceptable to the young people.

   Health promotion programmes have now been established in community homes. Packages of six-week blocks of group work have been offered to four community homes. Also individual health promotion work has been undertaken with the young people, including topics such as, drugs, sexual health, nutrition and first aid.

   Future plans include:

- establishing a focus group influenced by the young people themselves to guide the future development of the programme;
- appointment of a full-time mental health worker with fixed sessions in each community home (funding has been agreed, September, 1999);
- extending the programme to include young people in foster care; and
- developing written materials in a form of training manual along with the NCB.

This report was produced by Nottingham Community Health NHS Trust, Nottingham Healthcare NHS Trust, The University of Nottingham and Nottinghamshire County Council Social Services.

To obtain a copy of the full report contact: Raman Shukla, HYPCH Children's Services, Radford Health Centre, Ilkeston Road, Radford, Nottingham NG7 3GW.

'CARE SICK'? THE PHYSICAL AND MENTAL HEALTH NEEDS OF A SAMPLE OF YOUNG PEOPLE IN LOCAL AUTHORITY RESIDENTIAL CARE IN EDINBURGH

OBJECTIVE

With no local overview available, the aim of this study was to consider the perceived physical and mental health needs of a selection of looked after and accommodated (i.e. in care) young people within local authority residential units in Edinburgh and the possible effect of social exclusion on their access to health services.

This was a short research project funded by the Scottish Office Public Health and Inequalities Fund, carried out between February and July 1999 by a small research team based at the Young People's Unit (the Adolescent Mental Health Service covering Edinburgh, East and Mid-Lothian) at the Royal Edinburgh Hospital.

Method

Quantitative data for the study came from self-report, demographic and standardised questionnaire information obtained from 28 (of a possible total of 44) young people aged between 13 and 16 years in five residential units. (There is an overall total of 100 young people (aged 12–16) in residential units in Edinburgh.)

Qualitative data regarding the perceptions of the physical and mental health of the young people in residential care and issues relating to their access to services was obtained from five focus groups with accommodated young people ($n=20$) and five focus groups with residential staff ($n=34$). The findings were then presented at a local multi-professional seminar ($n=38$) and the results and action points generated were reported to the Scottish Office.

Results

Of the accommodated young people, 85% experienced severe levels of distress and psychosocial impairment. Forty-five per cent reported current physical health problems. Depression scores were 40% higher and rates of health-risk behaviours were considerably higher than community samples. Poor information, stigma, ambivalent beliefs and the marginalisation of residential care staff were some of a number of factors that affected access to health services.

Conclusion

The young people in our sample had major health concerns and needs that were not being adequately addressed because of a complex interplay of factors mainly intra-agency and inter-agency which reinforced their exclusion from appropriate services.

Peter Robinson, Katy Auckland, Helen Crawford and Charlotte Nevison

A summary copy of the full report can be obtained by contacting Peter Robinson, Research Fellow at the Young People's Unit, Royal Edinburgh Hospital, Tipperlinn Road, Edinburgh EH10 5HF.

Responsibility for looked after children

Mr Richard White

WHICH CHILDREN?

(Statutory references are to the Children Act 1989 unless otherwise specified.)
Local authorities look after children who:
- are in care that is subject to a care order; or
- are provided with accommodation in the exercise of an authority's statutory functions.

An authority is required to provide accommodation for children:
- removed on an emergency protection order;
- in police protection;
- detained under the Police and Criminal Evidence Act 1984;
- remanded under provisions of the Children and Young Persons Act 1969;
- made the subject of a supervision order with a residence requirement under the 1969 Act; or
- in need, where the terms of section 20 of the Children Act 1989 are satisfied.

WHO HAS PARENTAL RESPONSIBILITY?

It is important to know who has authority to exercise parental responsibility for the purposes of taking decisions about looked after children, including questions about consent to treatment. Circumstances can be complex, and in any case of doubt, legal advice should be sought.

Both parents have parental responsibility where they were married to each other at the time of the child's birth (s2). If they were not married at the time of the birth, the mother alone has automatic parental responsibility. The father can acquire responsibility by marrying the mother or by entering into a parental responsibility agreement with the mother or he may obtain a parental responsibility order from the court. Practitioners should be aware that the statutory provisions are under review and it may be that the law will be changed to give the father the same responsibility as the mother from birth. Married parents retain parental responsibility whatever other orders are made in respect of the child, unless the child is made subject to an adoption order or an order freeing a child for adoption. It is unusual for a father who has acquired parental responsibility to have it removed.

The definition of birth is extended to include the period from conception (Family Law Reform Act 1987, s1). In other words, if the parents were married at any time from conception, the father has parental responsibility.

Other persons may acquire parental responsibility. These are:

- a guardian appointed by a will or other document signed by a parent with parental responsibility to act from the death of that parent (subject to the powers of any surviving parent) (s5); and
- any person who obtains a residence order, for example a relative or foster parent, for the duration of the order, who will then share responsibility with the parent (s12).

Where a local authority is designated as the care authority in respect of a child, the authority has parental responsibility for the child (s33 (3)(a)), shared with the parent. In such a case, the authority has power to determine the extent to which a parent or guardian of the child may meet their parental responsibility (s33 (3)(b)), but this power may not be exercised unless the authorities are satisfied that it is necessary to do so in order to safeguard or promote the welfare of the child (s33 (4)).

A person or authority who obtains an emergency protection order acquires parental responsibility for the period of the order. The period cannot be for more than 15 days, and the responsibility may only be exercised in such a way as to safeguard or promote the welfare of the child with regard to the duration of the order (s44).

In no other case does a local authority have parental responsibility for a looked after child and it must therefore look to those with responsibility for decisions about the child's future. A person having responsibility may arrange for some or all of it to be exercised by someone acting on their behalf, but they may not surrender or transfer it. This may be appropriate where a local authority is looking after a child without a care order (s2(9)).

It remains important to consult a person with parental responsibility when considering any decisions about the child, and if necessary to obtain their consent to a course of action. Where more than one person has parental responsibility, each of them may act alone, subject to any court order, but it is good practice to consult all those having responsibility, if available, in respect of any important decision about the child's future.

One exercise of parental responsibility is to give consent to medical treatment.

CONSENT TO TREATMENT

Consent is the voluntary and continuing permission of the patient to receive a particular treatment, based on an adequate knowledge of the purpose, nature, likely effects and risks of that treatment including the likelihood of its success and any alternatives to it. Permission given under any unfair undue pressure is not 'consent'. (Mental Health Act Code of Practice, 1999)

In the case of any young person, it is necessary to consider who is capable of giving the required consent. A person having parental responsibility can give consent on behalf of a young person. Where the young person is subject to a care order, the consent of the local authority may be sufficient. In the case of a young person who is 16 or 17, their consent "shall be as effective is it would be if he were of full age; and where a minor has... given an effective consent to any treatment it shall not be necessary to obtain any consent for it from his parent or guardian".[1] If the young person is looked after by a local authority but subject to a care order, the authority may not consent on their behalf, unless a person having parental responsibility has delegated it to the authority.[2] In the case of a young person under 16, if the person carrying out the treatment considers that the young person has sufficient understanding to give an informed consent, that consent may be relied upon.[3]

If the person having parental responsibility declines to exercise it, or, where the young person who is 'Gillick-competent' refuses necessary treatment, those concerned for the safety and welfare of the young person will have to consider whether further steps should be taken. Where a competent young person refuses to consent, but the adult having parental responsibility consents, that acts as lawful authority for the treatment. Even if there is a proper consent, it may still be desirable to seek a court order to provide an opportunity for arguments to be considered on behalf of the young person. If there is no consent, a court application may be necessary. If the young person is likely to suffer significant harm in a general sense, it may be appropriate for a local authority to seek a care order.[4] If the care of the young person is generally adequate, it may be appropriate to seek a specific issue order.[5] Such cases can be complex and legal advice should be obtained.

Although there are specific circumstances provided for in the Children Act relating to short-term court orders, where a young person may refuse to be assessed or treated, their refusal can be overridden by an order of the High Court.

Note

This area of the law is fluid and practitioners should ensure that they are informed of latest developments.

Key Reading

Black, D., Harris-Hendricks, J. & Wolkind, S. (1998) *Child Psychiatry and the Law*. London: Gaskell.

---

1. Family Law Reform Act 1969, s8(1).
2. Section 2(9). Delegation should be in writing.
3. Gillick *v* West Norfolk and Wisbech Area Health Authority (1986) AC 112, from which comes the phrase 'Gillick-competent'.
4. Under s31.
5. Under s8. Any interested party may, with the consent of the court, seek this order.

Contact details for the 24 Mental Illness Specific Grants

(For further information and for more up-to-date details visit YoungMinds website: www.youngminds.org.uk)

Brighton and Hove: Attachment Project
Fiona Johnson, Brighton and Hove Social Services Blakers House, 79 Stanford Avenue, Brighton BN1 6FA.
Tel: 01273 295684; Fax: 01273 295392.

Bury and Rochdale: Bury Home and School Support Project
Sue Myers, Bury Social Services, HASSP Team, 65 Fir Street, Ramsbottom, Nr Bury, Lancashire BL0 0BG.
Tel: 01706 829453; Fax: 01706 8294531.

Christina Scarborough, Rochdale Social Services, Child and Adolescent Unit, Birch Hill Hospital, Birch Road, Rochdale, Lancashire O42 9QB.
Tel: 01706 755925; Fax: 01706 755105.

Cheshire: CAMHS Project
Lesley Goode (covering Crewe), Children's Outreach Services, Stable Block Boothville, London Road, Sandbach, Cheshire CW11 3BF.
Tel: 01270 759722.

Geoff Mount (covering Ellesmere Port), Poole Centre, New Grosvenor Road, Ellesmere Port, Cheshire CH65 2HB.
Tel: 0151 356 2763; Fax: 0151 348 1605.

City of York and North Yorkshire: School Based Support Project
Sue Milne, CAMHS (York), Ashbank, 1 Shepton Road, York YO30 5RE.
Tel: 01904 555616; Fax: 01904 555602.

Ken Dennis, c/o The Close, 58 North Allerton Road, Brompton, North Allerton, North Yorkshire DL6 2QH.
Tel: 01609 779922; Fax: 01609 778906.

Cornwall: Behavioural Support Programme
Helen Ferris, Divisional Manager, Social Services, 4 Carlyon Road, St Austell, Cornwall PL25 4NG.
Tel: 01726 63582; Fax: 01872 327 468.

Derby City: Derby Bridge Project
John Parr, Bridge Project, Kingsmead Centre, Bridge Street, Derby DE1 3LB.
Tel: 01332 716017; Fax: 01332 716013.

Devon
Martin Spragg, Youth Offending Team – Exeter, 45 St Davids Hill, Ivybank, Exeter EX4 4DN.
Tel: 01392 382000; Fax: 01392 384985.

Dorset: Connections
Katrina Gall, The Children's Centre, Damers Road, Dorchester, Dorset DT1 2LB.
Tel: 01305 259460; Fax: 01305 299461.

Essex
Andy Quin, Essex County Council, PO Box 11, County Hall, Chelmsford, Essex CM1 1LX.
Tel: 01245 434808; Fax: 01245 450437.

Leicester/Leicestershire/Rutland: Child Behaviour Intervention Initiative (CBII)
Joe Dawson (covering Leicester City), Educational Psychology Service, Leicester City Council, Collegiate House, College Street, Leicester LE2 0JX.
Tel: 0116 255 5051.

Sam Lloyd (covering Rutland), Partnerships Manager, Rutland County Council
Social Services and Housing Department, Catmose, Oakham LE15 6HP.
Tel: 01572 758324; Fax: 01572 758307.

Rob Wakefield (covering Leicestershire County), Senior Case Worker, Leicestershire County Social Services Department, Hinckley Social Services Office, 27 Upper Bond Street, Hinckley, Leicestershire LE10 1RH.
Tel: 01455 636964; Fax: 01455 250450.

Lewisham: ARTService
Catherine Duffy, Service Units Manager, ARTService, Ashby Road Centre, 1–3 Ashby Road, London SE4 1PR.
Tel: 020 8314 9137; Fax: 020 8314 3462.

Michael Jenkins, Team Administrative Officer, ARTService
Ashby Road, London SE4 1PR.
Tel: 020 8314 9742; Fax: 020 8314 3462.

Liverpool: The Rosta Project
Toby Biggins, Director, c/o Child and Family Services: NE Team, Alder Hey Children's Hospital, Eaton Road, Liverpool L12 2AP.
Tel: 0151 252 5217; Fax: 0151 252 5076.

Newham: Outreach Counselling Service for Young Asian Women
Madeleine Knowles, Social Services, London Borough of Newham, 16 Wordsworth Avenue,

Manor Park, London E12 6SU.
Tel: 020 8503 5825; Fax: 020 8557 8906.

Norfolk: Norfolk Family Support Teams
Dawn Gregory, Norfolk Family Support Team, Norfolk Social Services Department, Carrow House, King Street, Norwich NR1 2TN.
Tel: 01603 223500; Fax: 01603 223513.

Northamptonshire: Delta Project
Jane Roebuck, Northampton Social Services, Commissioning, Planning and Policy, County Hall, PO Box 177, Northampton NN1 1AY.
Tel: 01604 237149; Fax: 01604 237600.

Sheffield: Support Service for Looked After Children
Deborah Moore, NSPCC, Rivermead Unit, Herries Road, Northern General Hospital, Sheffield S5 7AU.
Tel: 0114 243 4343.

Southampton: Behaviour Resource Service
Susan Allen, Behaviour Resource Service, Social Services, 52 Seagarth Lane,
Shirley, Southampton SO16 6RL.
Tel: 01703 775610; Fax: 01703 701759.

Jane Martin, Project Manager, Behaviour Resource Service, Social Services, 52 Seagarth Lane, Shirley, Southampton SO16 6RL.
Tel: 01703 755610; Fax: 01703 701759.

Southwark: The Care Link Project
Christine Cocker, Southwark Social Services, Children's Services Direct,
Dulwich Office, 47b East Dulwich Road, East Dulwich, London SE22 9BZ.
Tel: 020 7525 4438; Fax: 020 7525 4449.

Staffordshire: Sustain Project
Deb Smith, Staff House One, The Old House, Eastern Avenue, Litchfield, Staffordshire WS13 7SQ.
Tel: 01543 510147; Fax: 01543 510147.

Tower Hamlets: Multi Agency Preventative Team (MAP)
Meena Hoque, Principal Manager, Specialist Services, London Borough of Tower Hamlets, Social Services, 62 Roman Road, London E1 0QJ.
Tel: 020 7364 2129; Fax: 020 7364 2266.

West Berkshire: Child and Adolescent Mental Health Project for Children Looked After or Victims of Abuse
Judith Williams, Principal Officer for Children, West Berkshire Social Services
Avonbank House, West Street, Newbury, Berkshire RG14 1BZ.
Tel: 01635 519734; Fax: 01635 519740.

West Sussex
Chris Scanes, Grange Block, County Hall, Chichester, West Sussex PO 19 1RT
Tel: 01243 777076; Fax: 01243 777324.

Other Mental Illness Specific Grants not mentioned in Part Two

Cambridgeshire: Integrated Support Project
Malcolm Turner, Service Development and Commissioning Officer (Mental Health), Cambridge Social Services, Room C003, Castle Court, Shire Hall, Cambridge CB3 0AP.
Tel: 01223 717912; Fax: 01223 718153.

Kay Sargent, (Evaluator of Project), Lecturer in Children and Families Social Work, School of Social Work, University of East Anglia, Norwich NR4 7TJ.
Tel: 01603 592068.

Aims to help all vulnerable children by ensuring a comprehensive and robust network of field, social work, family support services, CAMH assessment, primary care mental health workers and links with adult mental health services.

Leeds: 0–16 Team
Richard Chillery, 0–16 Team, East Leeds Family Learning Centre,
Brooklands View, Leeds LS14 6SA.
Tel: 0113 224 3317; Fax: 0113 224 3102.

Aims to help children and families experiencing child and adolescent emotional problems and parenting difficulties, through time-limited intervention to families, using a multi-disciplinary consultancy team to support Tier 1 staff.

Useful addresses

Action for Sick Children
1st Floor, 300 Kingston Road, London SW20 8LX.
Tel: 020 8542 4848; Fax: 020 8542 2424.
Website: www.actionfor sickchildren.org.uk
This charity monitors standards and provides support to parents with sick children. They provide a vital parent help line, information on children's health issues and guidelines for health professionals.

Barnardo's
Tanners Lane, Barkingside, Ilford, Essex IG6 1QG.
Tel: 020 8550 8822; Fax: 020 8550 6870.
Website: www.barnardos.ie
Barnardo's is the UK's largest children's charity. They have many services including: family centres, family placements, respite care, leaving care and juvenile justice.

Careline
Tel: 020 8514 1177 (Mon-Fri 10am–4pm, 7pm–10pm).
Confidential counselling for young people and adults. Can also refer callers to other organisations and support groups throughout the country.

ChildLine
Studd Street, London N1 OQW.
Tel: 0800 1111 (24 hours); Fax: 020 7239 1001.
Website: www.childline.org.uk

(For young people only)
Freepost 1111, London N1 0BR.
Tel: 0800 1111 (24 hours).
Provides confidential counselling, support and advice on any issue.

ChildLine for Children and Young People in Care
Freepost 1111, Glasgow G1 1BR.
Tel: 0800 884444.
A special free telephone line for children and young people who are looked after in children's homes, foster homes and residential care.

The Child Psychotherapy Trust
Star House, 104–108 Grafton Road, London NW5 4BD.
Tel: 020 7284 1355; Fax: 020 7284 2755.
E-mail: cpt@globalnet.co.uk
The Child Psychotherapy Trust is dedicated to improving lives of emotionally damaged children and adolescents by increasing access to child and adolescent psychotherapy services.

The Children's Legal Centre
University of Essex, Wivenhoe Park, Colchester, Essex CO4 3SQ.
Tel: 01206 872466 (admin); Fax: 01206 874026; Advice line: 01206 873820.
Website: www2.essex.ac.uk/clc; E-mail: CLC@essex.ac.uk
The Children's Legal Centre is an independent national charity dedicated to the promotion of children's rights. The centre runs a national legal advice line on all issues of law, policy and practice affecting children and young people.

The Children's Society
Edward Rudolf House, Margery Street,London WC1X 0JL.
Tel: 020 7841 4436; Fax: 020 7841 4436.
Website: www.the-childrens-society.org.uk; E-mail: info@the-childrens-society.org.uk
The mission of The Children's Society is to be a positive force for change in the lives of children and young people whose circumstances make them particularly vulnerable.

Coram Family (formerly The Thomas Coram Foundation for Children)
Coram Community Campus, 49 Mecklenburgh Square, London WC1N 2QA.
Tel: 020 7520 0300; Fax: 020 7520 0301.
E-mail: reception@coram.org.uk
The Coram Family works with vulnerable children and young people to promote resilience, enabling them to take responsibility for their own lives and achieve their full potential.

The Department of Health
Wellington House, 133–155 Waterloo Road, London SE1 8UG.
Tel: 020 7972 2000.
Website: www.doh.gov.uk
The Drug Education Forum
National Children's Bureau, 8 Wakley Street, London EC1V 7QE.
Tel: 020 7843 6038; Fax: 020 7278 9512.
The Drug Education Forum is working to achieve the provision of effective drug education for all children and young people in England.

Drugscope
32–26 Longman Street, London SE1 0EE.
Tel: 020 7928 1211; Fax: 020 7928 1771.
Website: www.drugscope.org.uk; E-mail: services@drugscope.org.uk
Drugscope has been created through the merger of the UK's foremost drug information and policy organisations: the Institute for the Study of Drug Dependence (ISDD) and the Standing

Conference on Drug Abuse (SCODA). Their aim is to infrom drug policy development and reduce drug-related risk. They provide quality drug information, promote effective responses to drug-taking, undertake research at local, national and international levels and advise upon policy-making.

FOCUS
The Royal College of Psychiatrists, College Research Unit, 6th Floor, 83 Victoria Street, London SW1H 0HW.
Tel: 020 7227 0821; Fax: 020 7227 0850.
Website: www.rcpsych.ac.uk/cru/crucurrent.htm
The FOCUS project aims to promote clinical and organisational effectiveness in CAMHS, with an emphasis on incorporating research into everyday practice.

The Health Development Agency (fromerly the Health Education Authority)
Trevelyan House, 30 Great Peter Street, London SW1P 2HW
Tel: 020 7222 5300; Fax: 020 7413 8900.
Website: www.hda-online.org.uk
The Health Development Agency (HDA) is a special health authority that aims to improve the health of people in England - in particular, to reduce inequalities in health between those who are well off and those on low incomes or reliant on state benefits.

The Joseph Rowntree Foundation
The Homestead, 40 Water End, York YO30 6WP.
Tel: 01904 629241; Fax: 01904 620072.
Website: www.jrf.org.uk
Independent, non-political body which funds programmes of research and innovative development in the fields of housing, social care and social policy.

The Mental Health Foundation
20–21 Cornwall Terrace, London NW1 4QL.
Tel: 020 7535 7400; Fax: 020 7535 7474.
Website: www.mentalhealth.org.uk; E-mail: mhf@mental health.org.uk
The Mental Health Foundation is working for the needs of people with mental health problems and those with learning disabilities. They aim to improve people's lives, to reduce stigma surrounding the issues and to promote understanding.

MIND
Mind Information Service, Granta House, 15–19 Broadway, Stratford, London E15 4BQ.
Tel: 08457 660163 (outside London) 020 8522 1728.
Website: www.mind.org.uk
Provides information on all aspects of mental health.

National Children's Bureau
8 Wakley Street, London EC1V 7QE.
Tel: 020 7843 6000; Fax: 020 7278 9512.

Website: www.ncb.org.uk
The NCB works to identify and promote the well-being and interests of all children and young people across every aspect of their lives.

National Children's Bureau
Children's Residential Care Unit, 8 Wakley Street, London EC1V 7QE.
The Children's Residential Care Unit Newsletter is published four times a year, highlighting current areas of research and projects as well as keeping people up-to-date with forthcoming events and publications. For general information on research projects at the CRCU, or sources of information on residential care issues.

National Children's Homes (NCH) Action for Children
85 Highbury Park, London N5 1UD.
Tel: 020 7704 7000; Fax: 020 7226 2537.
Website: www.nchafc.org.uk
NCH Action for Children aims to bring a better quality of life to Britain's most vulnerable children. The schemes under development are targeted at groups of young people who are disproportionately at risk of homelessness – young parents and young people from ethnic minorities. The aims are to create homes, to generate training and employment opportunities and to work with the young person's 'whole life' – their emotional needs as well as their practical ones.

National Pyramid Trust
204 Church Road, London W7 3BP.
Tel: 020 8579 5108.
The National Pyramid Trust aims to help vulnerable children achieve self-esteem, cope with school and succeed in life.

NSPCC
42 Curtain Road, London EC2A 3NH.
Tel: 020 7825 2500; Fax: 020 7825 2525.
Website: www.nspcc.org.uk; E-mail: infounit@nspcc.org.uk
The National Society for the Prevention of Cruelty to Children (NSPCC) is the UK's leading charity specialising in child protection and the prevention of cruelty to children.

The Place 2 Be
Edinburgh House, 154–182 Kennington Lane, London SE1 4EZ.
Tel: 020 7820 6487; Fax: 020 7735 8634.
E-mail: P2B@compuserve.com
The Place 2 Be aims to enable therapeutic and emotional support to be provided to children in schools based on a practical model backed up by research. Their aim is to promote positive mental health and well-being among primary school children thus reducing long-term problems.

Save the Children
17 Grove Lane, London SE5 8RD.

Tel: 020 7703 5400.

Website: www.savethechildren.org.uk

Save the Children is the UK's leading international charity, working to create a better future for children.

The Stationery Office (formerly HMSO)

The Publications Centre, PO Box 276, London SW8 5DT.

General enquiries: 020 7873 0011; Telephone orders: 020 7873 9090; Fax: 020 7873 8200. There are Stationery Office bookshops in various regional locations.

Voice for the Child in Care

Unit 4, Pride Court, 80–82 White Lion Street, London N1 9PF.

Tel: 020 7833 5792.

The VCC is a national network committed to improving the lives of children and young people in care. It provides a national advocacy service for children and young people in or leaving care.

The Who Cares? Trust

Kemp House, 152–160 City Road, London EC1V 2NP.

Tel: 020 7251 3117; Fax: 020 7251 3123.

Website: http://ww.thewhocarestrust.org.uk; E-mail: mailbox@thewhocarestrust.org.uk

The Who Cares? Trust are developing major programmes and campaigning hard to improve the lives of children in public care. It's their aim that these children realise their full potential, something which all children should have the chance to do.

YoungMinds

The National Association for Child and Family Mental Health, 102–108 Clerkenwell Road, London EC1M 5SA.

Tel: 020 7336 8445; Fax: 020 7336 8446.

Website: www.youngminds.org.uk; E-mail: young.minds@ukonline.co.uk

YoungMinds works to promote the mental health of children and young people. It aims to encourage the provision of accessible and effective services, to encourage public policy-makers to take account of the mental health needs of children and to make sure that the general public is more aware of these needs.

Youth Access

2 Taylors Yard, 67 Alderbrook Road, London SW12 8AD.

Tel: 020 8772 9900; Fax: 020 8772 9746; E-mail: yaccess@dircon.co.uk

Youth Access can give details and information of counselling services in the child or young person's local area.

Policy and practice update

Since this book first came out, a number of changes in policy, recommendations and new guidance in the area of looked after children have been announced by the Government. Material presented here aims to briefly update the reader on the latest policy and guidance.

POLICY AND GUIDANCE

The **Quality Protects** programme has been updated and now has 11 Government Objectives for Children's Social Services (Department of Health, 1999*a*). Initially, this was to be a 3-year programme; however, in November 2000 it was extended to a 5-year programme running to 2004. To support Quality Protects is the Children's Special Grant (Department of Health, 2000*a*). For further information regarding the 11 objectives and a database of good practice, visit http://www.doh.gov.uk/qualityprotects. The **National Priorities Guidance** enhances some of the objectives that have been addressed by Quality Protects with the addition of specific targets. These have also been updated (Department of Health, 2000*a*).

The **Connexions Service** has been set up as an inclusive service for every young person aged 13–19 who needs information, guidance, support or help with their personal development. A particular priority for the Connexions Service will be to make a difference to the life chances of vulnerable young people needing extra help to deal with barriers to learning and enable them to progress. Local authority Management Action Plans (MAPs) need to demonstrate that they are linked into the Connexions Service planning structure (Department of Health, 2000*a*; see http://www.connexions.gov.uk for further information).

Promoting Health for Looked After Children was released as a consultation document by the Department of Health (1999*b*). This provides general principles to meet the health care needs of children and young people as well as providing information and solutions on more specific issues regarding this population. As yet no final document has been published.

Guidance on the Education of Children and Young People in Public Care was published by the Department of Health and the former Department for Education and Employment (2000). This guidance emphasises the need for individual Personal Education Plans (PEPs), and recommends a 'designated teacher' to act as a resource and advocate for children and young people in public care.

Adoption: A New Approach is a White Paper (Department of Health, 2000*b*) that emphasises that more should be done to promote the wider use of adoption for looked after children who cannot return to their birth parents. A number of other routes to permanence have also been set out for looked after children.

The White Paper *Valuing People: A New Strategy for Learning Disability for the 21st Century* (Department of Health, 2001*a*) sets out Government proposals for maximising opportunities for children with disabilities and supporting young people's transition into adult life.

Following the proposals in the consultation document *Me, Survive. Out There?* (Department of Health, 1999*c*), the **Children (Leaving Care) Act 2000** came into effect in October 2001. The Act imposes new and stronger duties on local authorities to help care leavers until they are at least 21 years old, with an individual Pathway Plan and with a new financial regime (Department of Health, 2001*b*).

In February 2001, it was announced that a National Service Framework was to be developed for children's services, to make sure that every child has the best start in life. The **Children's National Service Framework** will develop new national standards across the NHS and social services for children (see http://www.doh.gov.uk/nsf/children.htm for further information).

Practice

A number of current initiatives provide examples of good practice in how mainstream services can provide interventions for this population. The NHS **Beacons Programme** is part of the Modernisation Agency whose main purpose is to improve health and social care by working in support of staff and managers in the NHS. In 2001 three new Beacons were announced in child and adolescent mental health. Two of these focused on work with looked after children. In 2002 three councils were awarded Beacon status for their adoption services (see http:// www.nhsbeacons.org.uk for up-to-date information on the NHS Beacons Programme).

The **Social Care Institute for Excellence** (SCIE) has been established by the Department of Health and the National Assembly for Wales and has an important role in spreading best practice and improving consistency in the quality of care. It is establishing a knowledge base for social care and developing guidelines about what works in practice and service delivery (see http:// www.scie.org.uk for further information).

References

Department of Health (1999*a*) *The Government's Objectives for Children's Social Services*. London: Department of Health.

—— (1999*b*) *Promoting Health for Looked After Children: A Guide to Healthcare Planning, Assessment and Monitoring* (consultation document). London: Department of Health.

—— (1999*c*) *Me, Survive, Out There?* London: Department of Health.

—— (2000*a*) *The Quality Protects Programme: Transforming Children's Services 2001–02*. Local Authority Circular LAC (2000) 22; Health Service Circular HSC 2000/033. London: Department of Health.

—— (2000*b*) *Adoption: A New Approach*. London: Stationery Office.

—— (2001*a*) *Valuing People: A New Strategy for Learning Disability for the 21st Century*. London: Stationery Office.

—— (2001*b*) *Children (Leaving Care) Act 2000: Regulations and Guidance*. London: Department of Health.

—— & Department for Education and Employment (2000) *Guidance on the Education of Children Looked After by Local Authorities*. London: Department of Health.

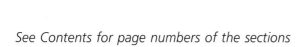

Index

See Contents for page numbers of the sections